Women, Partisanship, and the Congress

WOMEN, PARTISANSHIP, AND THE CONGRESS

JOCELYN JONES EVANS

First published in 2005 by
PALGRAVE MACMILLAN™
175 Fifth Avenue, New York, N.Y. 10010 and
Houndmills, Basingstoke, Hampshire, England RG21 6XS
Companies and representatives throughout the world.

PALGRAVE MACMILLAN is the global academic imprint of the Palgrave Macmillan division of St. Martin's Press, LLC and of Palgrave Macmillan Ltd. Macmillan® is a registered trademark in the United States, United Kingdom and other countries. Palgrave is a registered trademark in the European Union and other countries.

ISBN 1–4039–6662–1 hardback

Library of Congress Cataloging-in-Publication Data is available from the Library of Congress.

A catalogue record for this book is available from the British Library.

Design by Newgen Imaging Systems (P) Ltd., Chennai, India.

First edition: March 2005

10 9 8 7 6 5 4 3 2 1

Printed in the United States of America.

Contents

List of Tables   vii

List of Illustrations   ix

Acknowledgments   xi

1. Does Partisanship Impact Women's Legislative Behavior?   1

2. Does Partisanship Shape Women's Experience in the District?
    The Electoral Connection   21

3. Do Women in Congress Vote Alike? The
    Institutional Connection   51

4. Does Partisanship Shape Women's Participation
    in the Party Organization? The Organizational
    Connection   79

5. The Matrix of Women's Participation in Congress   123

Appendix   139

Bibliography   143

Index   155

List of Tables

1.1	The party culture thesis	10
1.2	The electoral security thesis	13
1.3	The matrix of member behavior based on party culture and electoral security	14
2.1	Routes to office of women serving in the house during the 107th Congress	29
2.2	Electoral returns across Congresses by party and sex	39
2.3	Average district presidential return across Congresses by party and sex	40
3.1	Mean ideological differences between male and female members across multiple measures in 2001	61
3.2	Predicting DW-NOMINATE scores of democratic members given electoral marginality	65
3.3	Predicting DW-NOMINATE scores of democratic members given female electoral marginality	67
3.4	Predicting DW-NOMINATE scores of Republicans given electoral marginality	69
3.5	Predicting DW-NOMINATE scores of Republicans given female electoral marginality	71
3.6	Mean party unity based on partisanship and sex of member: 1993–2001	73
4.1	Gender composition of the U.S. House: 103rd to 107th Congresses	91
4.2	Distribution of select positions among Democrats by sex	92
4.3	Distribution of select positions among Republicans by sex	96
4.4	Conference attendance by sex	101
4.5	Leadership PACs by sex: 105th to 107th Congresses	104
4.6	Media appearances by party and sex in 2000 and 2001	105
4.7	Predicting party unity by party in 2000 and 2001	108
A1	Variable descriptions and coding	139
A2	Classification of interviews	141

List of Illustrations

2.1   Percent of marginal members by party and sex:
      103rd to 107th Congresses   41
2.2   Mean DW-NOMINATE scores for the 103rd to
      107th Congresses by sex and partisanship   43
2.3   Mean DW-NOMINATE scores for the 103rd to
      107th Congresses by party, sex, and electoral security   45
5.1   Model of the Democratic system   131
5.2   Model of the Republican system   133

Acknowledgments

This book is the product of both instruction and experience made possible by so many people. I offer great thanks to the professors who contributed to my knowledge of legislative theory, without which conceptualization of this project would have been impossible. Largely responsible for the completion of this work is the staff and faculty of the Carl Albert Center for Congressional Research and Studies at the University of Oklahoma who provided me with the necessary support to conduct my research. In particular, my thesis advisor, Dr. Gary Copeland, was indispensable in the theoretical framework for this study. Additionally, the insights of Dr. Ron Peters, Dr. Ronald K. Gaddie, Dr. Jill Tao, and Dr. Carolyn Morgan proved essential to the development of the theoretical and methodological frameworks for the analysis.

Further, I offer my sincere gratitude to the practitioners who contributed to my understanding of the process of legislating. My experiences in the nation's capital through the American Political Science Association's Congressional Fellowship Program offered the opportunity to watch and record congressional politics firsthand. The fellowship also provided the access for my interviews of Members of the House of Representatives. The data offers a rich qualitative context to support the theoretical argument of the study. I also owe major thanks to one particular office, which not only allowed me the opportunity to work as an APSA congressional fellow in the House Republican Conference office, but also offered assistance in setting up interviews with other congressional offices on both sides of the aisle.

This book is also the product of immense support from my family. It is the product of others' confidence and investment in me. No other people had as much belief in me and my ability to accomplish "anything I set my mind to" than my parents. They have illustrated undying faith in my success. As my teacher, my mother instilled in me a commitment to learning. As a friend, she never stopped listening. My father ensured that I had all of the resources I needed to be the best student and teacher possible. He also provided me with the role model I needed to develop an interest in politics and envision a career in academia. This project is the product of their commitment.

Further, this research is the product of friendship and academic support. Without the encouragement of my colleagues at the University of Oklahoma, the University of Wisconsin-Green Bay, and the University of West Florida, this project would still be in a pile of papers on the living room floor. Special acknowledgment goes to Dr. Harvey Kaye, Dr. Kim Nielson, and Dr. Troy Abel for their many contributions—theoretical, methodological, and editorial—and for their professional support and help to see this project to publication. I sincerely thank the faculty, staff, and students of the department of government at the University of West Florida, namely Dr. Alfred Cuzán, Dr. Michelle Williams, Melissa Neal, and Ashley Traughber, who dealt with my frazzled state during the publication process. Your patience and support were indispensable. My graduate assistant, Jonathan D'Avignon, deserves eternal blessings for his patience and diligence in preparing this project for publication. Outside of the university setting I must acknowledge the editorial staff at Palgrave for helping me every step along the way as well as the anonymous reviewer for such insightful and thorough comments. It is a much better book because of you.

And finally, I owe more emotional support than I can ever repay to my husband, Jeremy Evans. His persistent reflections on this project as well as his unconditional support of my future goals and aspirations make him largely responsible for successful completion of this book. Together we make a great team. Thank you for loving me through everything.

Chapter 1

Does Partisanship Impact Women's Legislative Behavior?

The 106th and 107th Congresses were pivotal periods for women in both party organizations. In the Republican Party, Rep. Marge Roukema (R-NJ), the most senior Member on the Banking Committee, was passed over for the chairmanship. She retired at the end of the 107th Congress. During the same Congress, Rep. Nancy Pelosi (D-CA) ran for the leadership post of Minority Whip and won. After the congressional elections in November of 2002, Pelosi became the minority leader in the U.S. House of Representatives, replacing Rep. Richard Gephardt (D-MO). This party election installed her in the highest leadership office ever occupied by a female Member of Congress. Pelosi's ascension to power was provided through the vehicle of the party organization. Roukema's descent from power was also due to the structure of the party organization. Why was the Democratic Party the first to elect a woman to leadership? Why was the Republican Party averse to Roukema as committee chair? Why were they willing to sacrifice having a woman in such a prominent role of committee leadership?

In October of 2003, Deborah Pryce (R-OH), chair of the House Republican Conference, led a Congressional Delegation (CODEL) of congresswomen to Iraq. This delegation was touted as bipartisan, though its membership was largely Republican. Of the nine Members who went on the trip, two were Democrats. These two women represented military districts and suburbia. On Republican websites, the trip was broadcast as "Deborah Pryce, leader of the Republican Conference," while on Democratic websites, the trip was communicated as "women reach out to Iraq." Why the difference?

These two scenarios set the stage for the exploration of this book. Women operate in a complex world of party politics and personal gain. The focus of this project is to untangle the partisan dynamic of female Members' congressional behavior and understand its implications for female Members in achieving their personal and professional goals within Congress.

Introduction

While gender theory suggests stark differences between the sexes in terms of legislators' issue voting, committee behavior, and leadership styles, it offers little insight on possible ideological and behavioral differences among women in the Congress. Through an examination of ideological, partisan, and legislative behavior of women, this study provides a more thorough understanding of women's participation in the legislative arena. One of the nuances of this study is its attention to the informal structures of Congress.

Little work in the field of political science has been done to assess the partisan dynamic of electoral politics. Similarly, little has been done to capture female Members' involvement with and attitudes toward the political parties in terms of organizational and issue support. This analysis provides a look at the informal contexts including the electoral arena and the party organizations within which women participate as ideological and partisan actors.

Only a handful of studies of women's legislative behavior in the national arena have been conducted in the aftermath of the Republican takeover of the Congress. While some examinations include the 103rd Congress and the 104th Congress for purposes of comparison, very little work extends beyond these congresses. One of the most important contributions of this work therefore is the contemporary nature of the data. While interviews of Members of Congress, their staff, and other party elites were compiled during the 107th Congress, the quantitative data spans the 103rd through 107th Congresses, thus capturing a decade of legislative behavior and both Democratic and Republican control of the Congress.

The present analysis examines the participation of women in the U.S. House of Representatives within the context of political parties. At the electoral level, female Members face unique electoral circumstances due to their partisanship. Members representing the most liberal or conservative districts in the country enjoy wide electoral margins and great discretion to pursue the legislative, partisan, and personal goals that accompany them. Female Democratic Members largely represent the most Democratic districts in the country. Consequently, female Democratic Members enjoy great legislative discretion. Members representing the most moderate districts in the country have narrow electoral margins, competitive elections, and little discretion to pursue legislative, partisan, and personal goals in Congress. Female Republican Members often represent marginal districts with moderate constituencies and enjoy little legislative discretion.

In the U.S. House of Representatives, women demonstrate partisan patterns of ideological voting behavior. Democratic women vote like Democrats, and Republican women vote like Republicans. Partisanship shapes ideological voting in discernable ways. Republican women are not the same in ideological orientation as Democratic women; however Republican women are most likely to agree with Democrats on social issues, particularly women's issues (Swers 1998).

The electoral pressures faced by Republican women significantly affect their voting behavior. More electorally secure Republican women enjoy the legislative discretion to pursue their personal ideological preferences. They are significantly more liberal than both their Republican male colleagues and their electorally marginal Republican female colleagues. Marginal Republican women do not enjoy this legislative discretion. They vote as we might expect, based on both their gender and their electoral circumstance.

Although Democratic women illustrate higher party unity scores than their male colleagues, and Republican women illustrate lower party unity scores than their male colleagues, when examining the organizational behavior of women, we find that women participate in party-building activities to the same extent as men. Republican women attend organizational meetings, are affiliated with leadership Political Action Committees (PACs), and participate in media to the same extent as Republican men. Yet women in both parties lack proportionate representation at the highest levels of party and committee leadership. The Democratic Party rewards seniority, and thus women must serve the requisite time to reach these positions of power. In contrast, the Republican Party rewards party homogeneity and ideological loyalty, and thus women must demonstrate more conservative voting behavior to gain executive positions.

In the end, women participate in a legislative institution defined by political parties. These parties structure their behavior at the electoral, institutional, and organizational levels. In order to understand the implications of women's behavior within our Congress, we must account for the parameters created by partisanship and electoral circumstance. In the end, these party cultures determine the "playing field" on which women succeed or fail.

This book examines women's participation in the Congress at a time in history when women are the greatest in number in the U.S. Congress as well as at the highest level of leadership in this institution. It also explores and highlights the crucial differences between gender and ideology.

Additionally, it examines women's participation at a time when the most influential women in the policy debate are those in the majority party—that is, Republican.

A unique feature of this book is its diverse methods of analysis. First, it employs a dataset spanning ten years of congressional behavior, including the 103rd through the 107th Congresses (1992–2002). This decade-long dataset records the characteristics of congressional districts, legislative behavior, and institutional status of Members of the House of Representatives. Second, the findings of the book are drawn from anecdotal evidence as well as interview data from more than eighty Members of Congress, congressional staff, and party elites gathered during my tenure of over ten months as a congressional fellow in Washington, D.C. This experience allowed me to be a first-hand participant-observer, not only collecting primary data, but also gaining insight from behind-the-scenes encounters, conversations, and events. (For a discussion of the value of participant observation, see Fenno 1977; 1978.)

This introductory chapter presents the central focus of the study, places the work in theoretical context, and suggests the argument to be developed throughout the book. While many gender scholars have discovered differences in the political behavior of men and women, including their voting behavior, issue prioritization, and communicative style, very little work has been done to assess the role of partisanship or political parties in structuring these differences. This book focuses on the informal constraints posed by partisanship on women's political behavior within the U.S. House of Representatives. I understand women's participation in Congress to be structured by both their individual goals and their respective party culture. I argue that partisanship creates parameters that serve to constrain women's pursuit of their electoral and legislative goals in significant and meaningful ways. Consequently, after briefly examining the current research on women and politics, I explore two alternative theoretical frameworks of legislative behavior to explain the conduct of female Members. After establishing the theory driving the analysis, the introduction ends with a brief overview of the argument of the book as well as the content of the chapters to follow.

Women and Congressional Politics

It has long been noted that there are significant gender-based differences in the participation of male and female Members of Congress. Generally, female Members display more liberal voting records than male Members and are more concerned with "women's issues." Further, female Members have a different style of participation within the institution compared with male Members.

In general, women are better able to steer feminist policy through the policy process than congressmen because of their interest in effecting change and their desire to do so (Tamerius 1995; see also Thomas 1991). Social issues dealing with children, education, and welfare are thought to be rather soft issues appealing especially to female legislators (Thomas 1994, 1991). Women choose committees that tend to focus on more "feminine issues" (Thomas 1994). It is possible, however, that this choice is due to processes of gendered socialization that shape women's and men's interests in different ways and reflect the power and prestige these issues have within the legislative body (Kathlene 1994). Consequently, female public officials gravitate toward committees dealing with social welfare as well as family and children's issues out of interest, expertise, choice, coercion, or opportunity.

These observations lead theorists to the conclusion that women's increased inclusion in the Congress would lead to a more liberal voice on legislation, particularly on issues directly affecting women and children. They theorize that increased numbers of women in Congress would also change the political dynamic of the institution, increasing collaborative behavior among legislators and female leadership.

The present work challenges these implications on a number of grounds. Current gender theory tends to describe women's behavior as if it occurs in a political vacuum. Political parties are notably absent from theoretical models of gendered behavior. Gender theory has focused on the influence of gender on legislators' issue voting, participation as committee members, and behavior as party activists, to the neglect of possible ideological and behavioral differences among women. What has been the consequence? For the most part, the context of partisanship has been ignored. The purpose of the present analysis is to reintroduce partisanship into the theoretical picture. Specifically, this study focuses on the influence of partisanship on the participation of women in Congress. As Baer (1993) suggests:

> Research on women and politics has developed a narrow orthodoxy that has left the promise of the early gender-sensitive research of the 1970s stillborn, and an entire area of political science central to the political influence of women—political parties—has been both ignored and misunderstood. (548)

Consequently, current theoretical frameworks are unable to address differentiated ideological behavior in political organizations such as the legislative arena.

Similarly to Baer (1993), the contention of this book is that the neglect of political parties has formed a large hole in the literature on gender and legislative behavior in the Congress. Much of the gender literature tries to capture women's influence within the institution without taking into consideration the important function of partisanship in structuring Member behavior. Consequently, possible differences in women's behavior due to partisanship are left unexplored. Do Republican women behave the same way as Democratic women? Do they vote in the same way? Are their priorities the same? Do they have the same level of success within the institution? In other words, does gender alone determine legislative behavior, or does partisanship also influence the way in which women participate?

Political parties have always structured American politics. In the contemporary context, partisan competition is evident in every branch of our government. The need for a vote recount after the presidential election of 2000, the shift in partisan control of the Senate at the beginning of the 107th Congress, and the slim seat margins defining the House and the Senate since the midterm elections of 1996 all point to intense partisan competition in the contemporary era. As Swers (2002, 15) notes, "Policy is not made in a vacuum. Members are highly affected by the demands of their party caucus and leaders as well as the external political climate around them" (Rohde 1991; Cox and McCubbins 1993; Sinclair 1995).

Partisanship is not the only important factor of political context. Other factors such as Member goal motivations are also involved in determining legislative behavior. A substantial body of congressional theory suggests that Members are motivated by goals. First and foremost, Members are driven by the reelection incentive (Mayhew 1974a). Members are also motivated by more intra-institutional goals, such as policy, power, and prestige (Fenno 1973).

These goals are an important part of Member behavior that at present is also largely neglected by gender theory. Consequently, differences in women's political behavior due to electoral, policy, power, and prestige incentives are left unexplored. How does electoral vulnerability influence women's behavior? Do electorally vulnerable women act differently from electorally secure women? Do women motivated by institutional ambition act differently from women with less ambition? Are these goals associated in any way with partisanship? If so, not only must we understand the role of partisanship in women's political behavior, but also the role of goals in women's participation within the institution.

Placing Women's Legislative Behavior in Political Context

This analysis explores the behavior of women in the U.S. House of Representatives given the political context created by political parties and

Member goal-orientations. There are two primary assumptions of this work. First, the two primary political parties are distinguished by unique cultures that permeate the electoral, institutional, and organizational elements of our political system. Female Members, like male Members, participate within the parameters of these two political parties and reflect their distinctive cultures. Second, we can predict and understand Member behavior given that it is motivated by distinct, identifiable goals.

An argument original to this work, however, is that the pursuit of Member goals is structured by the party cultures. Women must conform to their partisan cultures in order to achieve their respective goals. In other words, if women expect to be effective legislators, they must adopt norms of behavior consistent with the cultures of their respective parties. From this theoretical foundation, we can develop models of Member behavior based on the interaction between party cultures and Member goals.

Party Culture

This analysis takes its point of departure from party culture theory, which suggests that the two parties demonstrate distinct patterns of behavior. Party culture theory challenges congressional scholars to consider partisan differences when examining legislative behavior. According to party culture theorists, "Because of these cultural differences the style of governance, as well as the content of policies, changes with a change in party control" (Freeman 2000, 12).

Republican Party culture is defined by ideological homogeneity, party loyalty, internal competition, hierarchical organization, and elite participation. "The Republicans have a unitary party in which great deference is paid to the leadership, activists are expected to be 'good soldiers', and competing loyalties are frowned upon" (Freeman 1986, 329). Some have labeled this style of governance a "top-down structure" in contrast to the Democratic leadership of decades past (Owens 1997). Evidence of Republican Party culture can be found throughout congressional politics. In the first days of the 104th Congress, after Republicans had gained leadership of the House of Representatives for the first time in forty years, Speaker Newt Gingrich embarked upon a revolutionary restructuring of the policies and procedures governing the House. Violating the long-standing tradition of the seniority rule, Speaker Gingrich bypassed Rep. John Myers (IN), Rep. Bill Young (FL), and Rep. Ralph Regula (OH), appointing the fifth-ranking Member on Appropriations, Robert Livingston (LA), as chair of the powerful committee (Aldrich and Rohde 1997, 549). Gingrich ignored the seniority rule in two other instances as well, appointing someone other than the ranking member as chair of Energy, Commerce, and Judiciary. " 'That was a strategic position,' explained one staffer for Majority Leader Richard Armey, 'and I think it ended up sending a very clear signal that you don't just rely on seniority; you've got to prove yourself as someone willing to pursue your agenda—or our agenda' " (Owens 1997, 250). While it is true that Democrats have ignored the seniority rule in appointments in decades past, this was not the only change in policy introduced by Speaker Gingrich. As Aldrich and Rohde (1997) suggest:

> Unlike the case of the Democrats twenty years earlier, this was not an instance in which pressure from freshman insurgents played a major role. This was clearly a leadership choice, imposed from the top after consultation. The decisions were announced by Gingrich and the top leadership. (550)

In addition, the leadership abolished three full committees and twenty-five subcommittees. Committee positions were reduced by 12 percent committee staff were reduced by a third; and committee and subcommittee chairs were limited to three terms. Further changes included the eradication of proxy voting, the elimination of seniority rule to select subcommittee chairs, and accountability of staff to full committee chairs (ibid.). Building on the structural changes to the Committee on Committees introduced by Republicans in the late 1980s to increase the control of leadership over the committee selection process, Gingrich further centralized control in the Committee in the 104th Congress, increasing the Speaker's voting power from 6 percent in the 103rd Congress to 17 percent in the 104th Congress (ibid.). In a final blow to the power of committees, Gingrich introduced a vast number of task forces to circumvent the orthodox legislative process and protect his sacred Contract with America.

This shift in the locus of power from subcommittees and full committees to party leadership marked a dramatic change in congressional politics. Not since the reforms of the 1970s had power been so centralized, and not since the speakership of Joe Cannon had a single leader exerted so much legislative control. Some scholars note that this new style of leadership closely approximates a responsible party model of government—one in which a political party campaigns on a coherent platform, is elected on that platform, and uses its power to enact that platform once elected (Committee on Political Parties 1950; Riley 1995).

Underpinning central leaders' insistence on both deadlines and legislative content was the new universally recognized condition of committee leadership in the new Republican-controlled House: that the majority party had a specific policy agenda, which they had put to the electorate and which the electorate had approved; that committee chairs were above all representatives of the majority party—not leaders of semiautonomous units able to recommend legislation that conflicted with the Conference's wishes—and that, should committee chairs err any significant distance from the party's wishes, Gingrich could invoke Conference rules at any time, call a meeting of the Steering Committee, and recommend removal of a chair (Owens 1997, 257–258).

While some things have changed about the way Republicans conduct business without Gingrich as their leader, the majority of the reforms remain intact. Speaker Hastert has significantly reduced the use of task forces to shield legislation from committee revision. Further, he has engaged in active listening, holding regular consultations with rank and file Members over major legislative initiatives. One of the major trends that have remained, though its cause perhaps has changed, is the focus in the Republican Party on teamwork and party loyalty. Speaker Hastert invokes sports imagery when rallying the party membership, encouraging them to think of him as their "coach"—the coach of a competitive team that must work together in order to win policy initiatives with such a slim majority (Andres 1999).

While leadership style has changed over the past ten years, Republican party culture has remained the same. Hastert's style works because the Republican rank-and-file has a culture of trust and deference to leadership. While sanctions are always available to Republican leadership, they are rarely used because of this habit of loyalty (Owens 1997).

There is evidence to suggest that this party culture permeates not only the national party organization, but also its affiliate organizations. The charter to the National Federation of Women's Republican Clubs (NFWRC) depicts this party culture in its stated purposes, approved January 1, 1938:

- To foster and encourage loyalty to the Republican Party and the ideals for which it stands.
- To promote education along political lines.
- To encourage close cooperation between independent groups and the regular party organization which are working for the same objective, namely sound government. To promote an inter-change of ideas and experiences of the various clubs to the end that any policies which have proved particularly effective in one state may be adopted in another.
- To foster, in the broad sense, uniformity of purpose and ideals.
- To encourage a national attitude and national approach to the problems facing the Republican Party. (Williams 1962, 11)

Apparent from these principles is a focus on party loyalty, ideological and purposive uniformity, and national leadership. The basic characteristics of Republican Party culture is depicted in table 1.1.

Table 1.1   The party culture thesis

Democrats	Republicans
• minority coalition-building conception of representation	• unitary conception of representation
• emphasizes individual group interest	• emphasizes national interest
• highly pluralistic structure	• highly elitist structure
• emphasis on group loyalties leading to ideological diversity	• emphasis on party loyalty leading to social and ideological homogeneity
• open and confrontational party politics	• closed and consensual party politics
• organizational style best reflected by social movement with discretion spread among different vocal groups	• organizational style best reflected by corporation with discretion at the top
• rewards seniority	• rewards party loyalty and party-building activities

By contrast, Democratic Party culture is defined by ideological as well as descriptive diversity, constituent responsiveness, seniority rule, and egalitarian organization and participation. "Essentially, the Democratic Party is pluralistic and polycentric. It has multiple power centers that compete for membership support in order to make demands on, as well as determine, the leaders" (Freeman 1986, 329). Informal groups within the Democratic Party such as the Congressional Black Caucus have been found to be even more loyal or unified to the group than to their regional or state party delegations (Pinney and Serra 1999). This unity has not decreased since the Republican takeover of Congress, suggesting that it is not just an artifact of majority party control.

Some have attributed this decentralized structure to the organizational reforms implemented by the national Democratic Party after the 1968 presidential election. The party implemented a new delegate selection process that in effect created a group-based form of politics. According to Hale (1995), the selection of delegates by demographics, the abolition of the unit rule, and the open nomination campaign process that empowered already organized groups, all led to a factionalized Democratic Party (see Shafer 1988). In 1982 the Democratic National Committee actually sanctioned this form of politics by formally recognizing seven intraparty caucuses: women, blacks, Hispanics, Asians, gays, liberals, and business/professionals (Elving 1988, cited in Hale 1995). Hale finds that these disparate groups used the national convention to vie for platform space but had little interest in building a unified liberal party message, and lacked the ability to do so (Hale 1992, cited in Hale 1995). This party climate has continued since the 1960s, with Democrats needing "to define a more general vision from the clash of competing factions" (Pomper 1985, cited in Hale 1995). As Hale states:

> Liberal Democrats since 1968 have been more a collection of groups representing some salient characteristic (labor, education, African Americans, Hispanics, women, homosexuals) or issue concern (anti-war, welfare rights, environmental, consumer, gun control, anti-nuclear, nuclear freeze, abortion rights) than a self-conscious ideological faction. This group-based politics did not produce a broader group identity out of which might grow a coherent liberal message and agenda for the party. (Hale 1995, 231)

Just as affiliated Republican organizations demonstrate a distinctive party culture, so too do Democratic organizations. The Democratic counterpart to the NFWRC is the Women's National Democratic Club (WNDC) that was founded in 1922. A separate wing of the organization, the Women's National Democratic Club Public Policy Committee, engages in policy advocacy. This committee is further divided into a series of task forces that focus on specific sets of issues. While the bylaws or founding principles of the WNDC are not stated anywhere on the organization's website, the Public Policy Committee serves a number of specific purposes. The committee:

- Advocates the role of women in the political process.
- Endorses economic and political equity and reproductive rights.
- Actively supports Democratic candidates for public office.
- Coordinates activities with the Democratic National Committee and other organizations with compatible goals.
- Publishes e-mail Action Alerts and the monthly Political Dispatch (http://www.democraticwoman.org/public_policy/. Accessed on January 1, 2004).

These purposes reflect the focus of the Democratic Party culture on descriptive diversity, constituent responsiveness, and organizational and participatory egalitarianism. table 1.1 summarizes the party culture thesis of the Democratic Party.

This book is novel in that it combines a database spanning a full decade of congressional behavior with personal interviews of Members of Congress and their staff to assess the manifestations of party culture in political behavior, and particularly women's political behavior. Both district-level and Member-level measures demonstrate partisan differences in Member voting behavior. The interview data further substantiates these findings demonstrating that women do define themselves as partisans and do operate within the political context and confines of their party organizations.

Partisanship structures the electoral circumstance of women, and thus influences their voting behavior, allocation of resources, prioritization of goals, and participation in partisan activities. Partisanship is further associated with male Members' attitudes toward and evaluations of their female partisan colleagues within the institution. Interestingly, while Democratic male and female Members articulate gender differences, these differences are not apparent in their voting behavior. Contrastingly, while Republican male and female Members do not articulate gender differences, there are significant gendered differences in their voting behavior.

Goal Motivations

Not only does party culture structure the context in which women participate in congressional politics, Members' personal goals also structure their participation. Members are driven by need for reelection. Some have even called them "single-minded seekers of reelection" (Mayhew 1974a). Others suggest that Members are driven by a number of identifiable goals. They are driven by policy, power, and prestige goals (Fenno 1973, 1977).

While reelection is the proximate goal, it serves to provide Members with the opportunity to achieve their other personal goals, such as policy priorities, power within the Congress or beyond, and prestige or fame as an effective politician. Parker (1992) suggests that Members try to expand their electoral security to attain the discretion or freedom necessary to pursue their institutional goals. Members expand their "electoral security" by increasing the percentage of the district vote they receive in each biennial election. The oft-cited incumbency advantage is evidence of Members having perfected the art of expanding their electoral security. As discussed in the first chapter, table 1.2 illustrates the electoral incentive argument.

A Matrix of Member Behavior

While women do influence legislative politics, their participation in Congress is mediated by a number of considerations. The position of women within the institution, such as their committee and leadership positions, as well as their relationship with their party organizations inside and outside of Congress, can impact their effectiveness in translating policy goals or preferences into legislative outcomes (Swers 2002). This book specifically explores how partisanship structures the attainment of Member

Table 1.2   The electoral security thesis

Secure Members	Marginal Members
• can spend less time and effort on district issues	• must spend more time and effort on district issues
• have more discretion to vote contrary to district preferences	• have less discretion to vote contrary to district preferences
• enjoy time necessary to pursue leadership positions and get involved in the party organization	• lack time necessary to pursue leadership positions and get involved in the party organization
• congruence of policy preferences with district and/or party organization	• less congruence of policy preferences with district and/or party organization

goals, including the basic goal of reelection. Reciprocally, this study demonstrates how goal motivations for Republicans can impinge upon female Members' participation in the party organization, thus limiting their institutional effectiveness. Parties have substantial powers that affect members' attainment of personal goals. As Aldrich and Rohde explain:

> Powers related to member incentives include rewards and punishments. The wider the range of these two kinds of inducements that leaders control, the more likely it is that they will be able to influence members' choices. Regarding punishments, parties can increase the influence their leaders or their caucuses have over the retention of positions of power. (2000, 4)

Table 1.3 illustrates how party culture combines with electoral security to create a matrix of Member behavior.

For Democratic Members, electoral security provides them the freedom to pursue personal goals, whether they involve power, policy, or prestige. Electoral security is usually associated with seniority, and this seniority provides Democratic Members with institutional status and the partisan leadership positions that accompany it. Electorally marginal or vulnerable Democratic Members, on the other hand, lack electoral discretion, and thus must focus their attention on district concerns. It is important to recognize that their partisan culture allows them the discretion to vote and participate in the interest of their districts. They are limited, however, within the institution because of their lack of seniority, but with time they can expect all the advantages that seniority brings.

Republican Members, in contrast, face altogether different circumstances within this framework. Electorally secure Republicans enjoy the freedom to pursue their personal goals, but they must pursue them within

Table 1.3 The matrix of member behavior based on party culture and electoral security

Party culture	Secure Members	Marginal Members
Democrats	• enjoy electoral and partisan discretion	• lack electoral discretion, but enjoy partisan discretion to vote in the interest of the district
	• enjoy seniority and the leadership positions that accompany it	• lack seniority and the leadership positions that accompany it
Republicans	• enjoy electoral discretion, but lack partisan discretion	• lack both electoral and partisan discretion to vote in the interest of the district
	• enjoy seniority but still must compete for leadership positions	• lack seniority and must compete for leadership positions

the parameters of the party platform in order to be effective within the organization. Seniority plays little role outside these party parameters. Even the most senior Members can expect to be overlooked for leadership positions if they do not conform their personal pursuits to the party platform. Electorally marginal Republican Members, while compelled to operate within this system of ideological and participatory homogeneity, lack the freedom to ignore district interests. In order to secure their reelection, they must occasionally stray from the partisan fold. Not only do they not adhere to the party platform, they also lack the personal or partisan resources to compete for leadership positions.

From this analysis, we develop a much richer understanding of Member behavior than that currently offered by congressional studies or gender literature. We understand Members as operating in a complex, dynamic legislative arena, both structuring and structured by their participation in it. We see party organizations truly as mediating institutions that not only impact Members' voting behavior, but also impact their behavior both inside and outside of Congress. Further, we appreciate parties as the professional and central organizations that they are, inherently structuring Members' goals of power, policy, and prestige. Specifically, we develop a critical understanding of the role of parties and partisanship in structuring women's political participation within the Congress. The two party cultures serve both to advance and to limit women's access to political power in contemporary congressional politics.

Note on Research

The data for this project was collected during the first session of the 107th Congress. As an American Political Science Association Congressional Fellow, I worked for a Member of the U.S. House of Representatives in Washington, D.C. from January to October of 2001. Not only did this experience offer me the unique opportunity to be a participant observer (Fenno 1990), I was also able to gain access to a number of congressional offices on both sides of the aisle for interviews with Members and their staff. For a detailed discussion of the interview data, please refer to the Appendix.

This study incorporates the findings of these interviews with a specially created dataset combining descriptive information (e.g., party affiliation, biological sex, and seniority), district information (e.g., socioeconomic character, district partisanship, vote return for the Member in the previous election), and behavioral characteristics (ideological orientation of roll-call voting) of Members of Congress. These two sets of data are integrated to varying degrees throughout the text to develop the argument of the book appropriately. The interview data serves to put a human face to much of the statistical findings of the chapters. Note that this research incorporates a variable to account for biological sex, but for stylistic reasons refers to the variable as gender. The author recognizes the substantive differences in these two terms, but sacrifices specificity for ease of interpretation.

One of the greatest contributions of this work is its combination of quantitative and qualitative data. The data set for this project spans ten years (1992–2002) and five congresses (103rd to 107th Congresses). It integrates district-level census data and electoral vote returns with Member-level data, such as the gender, party affiliation, and seniority of the Member, in order to control for situational factors in predicting ideological voting behavior. The quantitative data included descriptive Member indicators, such as the Member's gender and party affiliation, as well as district indicators, such as the vote return for the Member as well as the president in the last election (1992 or 1996). The gender of the Member was coded one for female and zero for male. The party affiliation of the Member was coded one for Republican and zero for Democrat, and Independents were excluded from the analysis. These descriptive indicators were taken from *The National Journal's Almanac of American Politics* (1994–2002). Electoral marginality of the Member was also taken from this source and was coded as the percent of the vote received by the Member multiplied by 100 for ease of interpretation. The variable was then coded dichotomously throughout the analysis, with vulnerable Members coded as those receiving less than 60 percent of the district vote, and safe Members coded as those receiving 60 percent of the vote or more.

The qualitative data incorporates interview data with organizational records to more fully capture the complex partisan environment in which Members operate. The interview data includes twenty-five Member interviews, forty-seven congressional staff interviews, and nine party elite interviews—a total of eighty-one interviews. The qualitative data for this chapter came from personal interviews of staff and Members in Washington, D.C. between June and December of the first session of the 107th Congress (2001). During the data collection for this analysis, the nation underwent a serious terrorist attack on September 11, 2001, that dramatically shifted the policy agenda and partisan mood. Fortunately, most of the interviews had already been conducted. There were, however, notable differences in the responses during the weeks immediately following September 11, 2001, from other interviews. During this period of bipartisanship, Members of both parties were less likely to discuss differences between themselves and their colleagues across the aisle. Nevertheless, due to the semi-structured nature of the interviews, most of the interview data mirror those gathered before this critical event. Certain direct references to the event are excluded from the analysis to provide a more consistent picture of Member behavior. All of these respondents provided me with information under the condition that their identities would not be revealed. Consequently, none of the respondents are identified by name or office in this work. In addition, any statements made during the interviews by Members that could serve as potential identifiers have been systematically excluded.

Along with congressional staff, I also interviewed staff of the political and organizational arms of the national parties, including: the House Republican Conference, the Democratic Caucus, the National Republican Campaign Committee, the National Federation of Republican Women, and an independent polling consultant hired to assist the Republican Party in its outreach efforts. The interviews were semi-structured, involving a series of open-ended questions concerning legislative priorities, group membership, campaigning, evaluations of the party organizations and personal roles, and perceived gender and partisan differences among colleagues.

Not only do I attempt to triangulate the data in the data set and the interviews to capture the full influence on Member behavior. I also recognize the significance of multiple measures of participation (Hall 1996). Analysis of Members' partisan participation within the district, within the Congress, and within the party organization more fully captures the relationship of party culture and legislative behavior. By examining women's legislative behavior at the electoral, institutional, and organizational level, we develop a more holistic understanding of female Members' political circumstances. Future studies of congressional behavior should attempt to bring together the disparate worlds in which Members operate.

As Fenno (1990) states:

> Politicians are both goal-seeking and situation-interpreting individuals . . .
> (They) act on the basis of what they want to accomplish in their world, and
> on the basis of how they interpret what they see in that world . . . (We) can
> gain valuable knowledge of their actions, perceptions, and interpretations by
> trying to see their world as they see it. (114)

The chapters of this book are set up to accomplish just this. Each chapter
examines a different arena in which Members participate. From the electoral arena to the congressional arena, and to the partisan arena, we find evidence of the partisan and goal matrix structuring women's legislative
behavior.

A Framework for Examining Women
as Partisans

One of the most widely accepted theories of congressional studies is that the
primary goal of Members of Congress is to win reelection. Beginning with
this fundamental motivation of congressional behavior, the reelection incentive, we first turn to the district to understand the role of partisanship.
In chapter 2, we examine the importance of district factors in understanding women's legislative behavior. It is here that the first constraints due to
partisanship are experienced. By combining the findings of interview data
with an analysis of electoral security, this chapter provides striking evidence
that Democratic women face an altogether different district dynamic than
Republican women. Democratic women represent some of the most liberal
and consequently the most secure districts in the Democratic camp. They
also belong to a party that permits Members to respond to district pressures
to secure reelection. By contrast, Republican women represent some of the
least conservative and consequently least secure districts in the Republican
camp. They also belong to a party that rewards party loyalty and thus limits
Members' ability to respond to district pressures. Republican women must
therefore balance their political ambition with their goal of reelection—a
trade-off that does not exist for Democratic women.

Chapter 3 addresses how these disparate district circumstances are
reflected in women's congressional behavior inside of the Congress. Are the
differences detected at the electoral level also evident at the institutional
level? Combining once again the findings of interview data with an in-depth
analysis of ideological voting behavior, we find that there are significant

differences in the behavior of female Members attributable to both partisanship and electoral security. In the end, although gender theory has largely assumed a cohesive women's voice concerning women's issues, there is reason to believe that women represent diverse constituencies that frame their preferences and behavior in different ways. Democratic women are much more formally unified with their party than Republican women. In addressing women's general ideological voting behavior, this analysis indicates that, for the most part, women act like partisans. The second major finding of chapter 3 is that partisanship shapes Members' voting behavior in discernable ways. First, Democratic party culture provides Members with freedom to respond to constituency pressures, whereas Republican party culture promotes loyalty and ideological homogeneity and does not provide Members with freedom to respond to constituency pressures. In other words, Republican party culture restricts the amount of freedom Members have to pursue goals, whether those be personal or constituent-driven. Consequently, Republicans do not respond to district pressures to the same extent as Democrats.

After finding that women act like partisans and that the parties demonstrate clear patterns of voting behavior and constituency responsiveness, chapter 4 turns to the informal behavior of women within the party organizations. In this chapter, four different forms of party-building activities are examined: attendance at party organizational meetings, status within party leadership, participation in the media, and association with leadership political action committees (or PACs). In conjunction with interview data, this analysis reaffirms the findings from chapters 2 and 3, and provides clear support for the notion of two very different party cultures in which women participate as legislators. While women of both parties participate in party-building activities to the same extent as men, Republican women's party-building activity is significantly associated with both their ideological behavior as well as their personal advancement within the institution. In contrast, Democratic women's party-building activities are not related to their ideological orientation or status within the party.

Chapter 5 brings together the analytical findings from chapters 2, 3, and 4 to provide support for and elaboration on the argument of the book. In sum, research presented in this book suggests that women participate within a complex matrix formed by both the partisan context and electoral goals of congressional behavior. These pressures result in an interesting dynamic where Republican women must balance district interests against personal advancement while Democratic women can pursue district interests and personal advancement simultaneously. The implications of these findings for women's representation are clear. While Republican women are in the best position to advance the interests of women, they are situated in a party culture that creates cross-pressures structuring their participation in the Congress. These pressures limit their ability to pursue the interests of women while advancing their status within the institution. On the other hand, Democratic women do not face cross-pressures that structure their participation, but they also do not enjoy the majority status necessary to advance their personal legislative goals. Understanding women's participation within the context of partisanship yields a much richer and more accurate picture of women's congressional behavior than previously provided by the literature.

At present, the political climate for women is intensely structured by partisanship. Women's participation within the institution largely depends on the status and cultures of the two major parties. These cultures permeate the electoral, institutional, and organizational aspects of the American Congress. In the electorate, party culture structures every aspect of campaigns and elections, determining both who runs and who wins. In the institution, party culture structures the committee system and the policy agenda, determining who has power and how they exercise it. Finally, party culture structures the party organizations in Congress, resulting in distinct leadership structures, roads to power, and modes of participation. We must understand the specific ways in which partisanship structures women's participation in order to begin to truly understand how women are making a difference within the American Congress.

Does partisanship impact women's legislative behavior? Indeed, women operate in a complex environment structured by partisanship. Their behavior is influenced by various cross-pressures, including party culture and electoral security. While Democratic women enjoy a party culture that facilitates constituency responsiveness and ideological diversity, Republican women operate within a culture that encourages party loyalty and ideological homogeneity. In the end, Republican women must make critical choices that influence their effectiveness within the party organization and thereby in the Congress. As long as the Republican Party holds the majority, the findings of this exploration have significant implications for the effectiveness of women within the institution and the representation of women at large. For students of politics, the argument that party culture structures Member behavior holds implications both theoretically and methodologically for the future study of congressional behavior. A pursuit of integrated theoretical frameworks and mixed methodologies is required to better understand the complex workings of the political environment in which women participate.

Chapter 2

Does Partisanship Shape Women's Experience in the District?
The Electoral Connection

She (Republican female Member) couldn't ever run for leadership because she's too busy securing her own race. But she would have been great (in leadership) because none of them are from vulnerable districts. She anticipates the train or the storm and would be a good spot check. If something is going to happen, she's the first to hear the rumbling.

— *senior staff for Republican female Member*

Introduction

This book examines the partisan contours of women's legislative behavior. Each chapter approaches the subject from a different perspective, including: the electoral circumstances of female Members within their district; the ideological nature of women's voting behavior within the institution; and the character of women's status and participation within the party organizations. In this section, we begin with the electoral connection to understand the different constituent pressures women face due to partisanship.

The legislative behavior of Members is first and foremost driven by reelection. While Members do have other motivations such as power, prestige, and policy development (Fenno 1973), they are fundamentally concerned with maintaining political office (Mayhew 1974; Fiorina 1977; Fenno 1978). The cause of this electoral connection is the structure of the American political system. Legislators are elected to represent the interests of their constituencies. For this reason, we should first look to the electoral connection for insight on the partisan contours of women's representation.

This analysis begins our quest from the vantage point of the district. We look to the electoral arena for insight on motivations for Member behavior. What do women see when they look to their districts? How do district pressures influence women's legislative behavior? Are there district pressures specifically related to partisanship that shape women's participation in the legislative arena?

A number of interviews with both Members and staff during the first session of the 107th Congress provide the qualitative data for this examination. Of the eighty-one interviews conducted for this research, twenty-five were with Members of Congress, forty-seven with congressional aides, and nine with party elites. All of these respondents provided information under the condition that their identity would not be revealed. Consequently, none of the respondents are identified by name or office in this work. From the vantage point of the campaign trail, respondents share their experiences and perspectives on the partisan arena in which female legislators must operate. The present chapter provides a rich context from which to formulate more adequate conclusions and implications concerning women's partisan behavior.

Legislative Behavior and the Electoral Connection

Some of the most influential theoretical works on the Congress, such as Richard Fenno's *Homestyle* (1977) and David Mayhew's *Congress: The Electoral Connection* (1974), point to the importance of the district and electoral politics to understanding a Member's legislative behavior. Members are well aware of the relationship between their voting behavior and their electoral safety. One incumbent interviewed by Fenno remarked: "[If] you get too far from your district, you'll lose it" (1978, 144). It is unlikely that one vote makes or breaks an incumbent's chance at reelection. A consistent divergence in a Member's general ideology from that of her district, however, can lead to incumbent vulnerability.

This analysis assumes that Members are concerned with reelection, and that they reflect the preferences of their constituents. Although findings are mixed (see Kuklinski 1977), the electoral marginality of a Member is somewhat associated with the Member's attentiveness to district concerns (MacRae 1958; Miller and Stokes 1963).

Consequently, the marginality thesis suggests that competitive districts are more moderate and thus Members representing these districts are more moderate in their ideological voting behavior (see Huntington 1950; Froman 1963; Erikson 1971; Fiorina 1974; Deckard 1976; and Sullivan and Uslaner 1978). Tests of this hypothesis have produced mixed results. While some have found electoral marginality to be associated with party disloyalty (Froman 1963), others have found disloyalty associated with higher electoral margins. Particularly for Republicans, those with the most diverse districts display partisan disloyalty that leads to higher rather than lower election returns (Deckard 1976). Those candidates who most closely match constituency opinion are more likely to win (Sullivan and Uslaner 1978). It is important to note that much of the seminal work on marginality finds partisan-based differences in the relationship between marginality and voting behavior (Froman 1963; Shannon 1968b; Deckard 1976).

For the purposes of this analysis, I examine the electoral security of Members as well as the general ideological climate of the district—another important influence on Member behavior (Bianco 1984; Bond, Covington, and Fleischer 1985; Canon 1990). Electoral security is measured as the percent of the vote received in the last election. The ideological character of the district is measured as the percent of the vote received by the winning presidential candidate in the last election. Why should we expect district variables to predict Member behavior? "Those representatives who grossly misjudge the empirical situation do not survive long in the electoral arena" (Fiorina 1974, 40).

The presidential vote return of a district is frequently used as a proxy to capture general district ideology. While this measure is the subject of debate, it is the most consistent data source available that measures voter preferences at the district level. Because it is based on voting behavior, it provides a more accurate indicator of the political character of the district than those provided by demographic characteristics (Bond, Campbell, and Cottrill 2001, 12). While some have used the mean presidential vote across multiple elections in order to limit the idiosyncratic effects of individual candidates (Bianco 1984), critics of this measure argue that doing so reduces the accuracy of the measure in capturing contemporary leanings (Bond, Campbell, and Cottrill 2001, 11).

Party Culture and Electoral Politics

Party structure is significantly related to the influence of women in the political process (Freeman 1986). While some have suggested that the Republican Party is a poor imitation of the coalition-building Democratic Party, the Republican Party is a different type of political organization with a different type of political culture altogether (ibid.). As presented in chapter 1, table 1.1 delineates the differences in party culture suggested by the literature (see Freeman 1986). The Democratic Party illustrates a highly pluralistic structure, whereas the Republican Party illustrates a more elitist structure. Freeman notes:

> Since the Democratic Party is composed of groups, the success of individuals whose group identification is highly significant, such as blacks and women, is tied to that of the group as a whole. They succeed as the group succeeds. That is not the case within the Republican Party. It officially ignores group characteristics. . . . Generally, individuals succeed insofar as the leaders with whom they are connected succeed. (336)

Consequently, the Republican Party advocates a more unitary conception of representation. Meeting the needs of national interest, such as improving the economy, is the appropriate means for meeting the needs of individual groups. On the other hand, Democrats hold a conception of representation that emphasizes minority coalition-building (ibid.). Freeman states:

> Democrats do not have an integrated conception of a national interest, in part because they do not view themselves as the center of society. The party's components think of themselves as outsiders pounding on the door seeking programs that will facilitate entry into the mainstream. Thus, the party is very responsive to any groups . . . (ibid., 338)

This ethos is further evidenced in the organizational style of the two parties. While Democratic party politics are often characterized as "open" and "confrontational," Republican Party politics are characterized as "closed" and "consensual" (ibid.). The organizational style of the Republican Party is best reflected by a corporation with discretion located at the top, whereas the organizational style of the Democratic Party is best reflected by a social movement with discretion located among the different vocal groups. The representational ethos and the organizational style of the Democratic

Party work hand-in-hand to produce an environment of conflict and change (ibid.).

One of the major consequences of these attitudinal and structural differences between the parties concerns the role of women within the parties. The Republican Party emphasizes loyalty to the party first and foremost, whereas the Democratic Party provides the vehicle whereby group loyalties may be articulated in the political arena.

According to Freeman (2000), "The year before the 1976 conventions, the National Women's Political Caucus (NWPC) organized a Republican Women's Task Force" of Ford supporters to promote the proposed ERA (Equal Rights Amendment) (Accessed from http://www.seniorwomen.com/articlesFreemanGone.html on June 6, 2002). Freeman (1986) suggests:

> Even in 1976, when Republican feminists were aligned with party leaders, one organizer commented that because the GOP is not "an interest group party . . . the RWTF (Republican Women's Task Force) is viewed with skepticism. Party regulars have a hard time adjusting to the presence of an organized interest." The current leadership views feminist organizations as Democratic party front groups. Thus it is virtually impossible to be both an accepted Republican activist and an outspoken supporter of feminist goals. Since the party discourages people from identifying themselves as members of a group with a group agenda, it minimizes the possibility of multiple loyalties. (348)

Another consequence of the Republican emphasis on party loyalty is widespread trust among rank-and-file Members of the Republican Party. An emphasis on social and ideological homogeneity fosters a trust of others within the group. Party leaders are thus capable of maintaining discretion over the policy agenda because they benefit from a large degree of membership trust (ibid., 351).

The extent to which the Republican Party changed both ideologically and structurally during the 1994 election and the 104th Congress thereafter remains a question for future scholarship. In predicting the 1994 election, Connelly and Pitney (1994) suggested that the Republican Party would need to "appeal to disparate constituencies and yet [be] unified enough to present coherent alternatives" (578). In retrospect, it appears the Republican Party has managed to maintain a substantial amount of loyalty while integrating a number (small as it may be) of demographically diverse legislators into its membership. This leads us to conclude that while conservative women have influenced the legislative debate, they have done so within the confines of partisan politics.

Women and the Electoral Connection

In order to explain the significant disparity between the number of male and female elected officials in national politics, gender theorists have devoted some attention to the electoral connection. Three different aspects of campaigns and elections have been thought to contribute to women's success as political candidates. First, research has focused on differences in the political ambition of men and women. Second, research examines differences in the way in which male and female candidates both perceive themselves and are perceived by the electorate. Finally, research measures how successful women are in terms of various campaign activities in vying for political office.

Early investigations on the subject of political ambition revealed significant differences between men and women (Bledsoe and Herring 1990; Constantini 1990; Dodson and Carroll 1991; Carroll 1994; Darcy, Welch, and Clark 1994; NWPC 1994; Fox 1997). The implications for gender theory were that women have less political ambition and thus are less likely to participate in national electoral politics (Carroll 1994; NWPC 1994). In light of "The Year of the Woman" (1992) and the electoral gains women made during the 1990s both at the state and local levels and at the national level (Cook, Thomas, and Wilcox 1994; Thomas and Wilcox 1998), recent research has revealed that the ambition gap is closing. Fox, Lawless, and Feeley (2001), in their examination of the interaction between gender and the decision to run for office, for example, find equal levels of political ambition among men and women.

While men and women might demonstrate equal levels of ambition in the contemporary context, there is evidence to suggest that they face unequal campaign environments. Female candidates feel a greater need than male candidates to establish their credibility when presenting themselves to the public (Fowler and McClure 1989; Kahn 1996). Perhaps, this perception is related to the finding that, given equal qualifications, men are much more likely to be encouraged to run for political office than women (Fox 1997).

Beyond credibility, women also face gendered stereotypes in the electorate. Male and female candidates are treated differently both by the media and by voters. In covering campaigns, the press does differentiate between male and female candidates by paying less attention to women than men when discussing issues (Kahn 1996). In terms of voter evaluations, female candidates appeal to female voters. In evaluating both House and Senate races, female voters are more likely to support female candidates than male voters. When there is a female candidate, female voters are also more likely to vote based on gender-related issues (Dolan 1998). Women are viewed as more liberal on social issues. These stereotypes do not necessarily disadvantage women. Especially in gubernatorial campaigns, sex stereotypes produce positive evaluations of female candidates (Kahn 1994). Consequently, the strong female candidates can often attract cross-over votes or votes from the other party (Zipp and Plutzer 1985). In other words, these sex stereotypes can draw moderate voters from the opposition party.

In light of both positive and negative gendered stereotypes, women appear to be enjoying equal levels of electoral success. Particularly in open seat elections, women of both parties fare just as well as men (Gaddie and Bullock 2000). Recent research suggests that female candidates are not disadvantaged in terms of fundraising and vote totals (Wilhite and Theilmann 1986; Leeper 1991; Burrell 1994, 1998; Darcy, Welch, and Clark 1994; Seltzer, Newman, and Leighton 1997). Low levels of female representation in the national political arena is due to gendered differences in the decision to run for political office rather than the success of female candidates in the electoral arena (Fox, Lawless, and Feeley 2001).

Although it is true that females of both parties are more likely to vote for female candidates, Democratic female candidates are most advantaged by the female vote because of their clear feminist stance (Plutzer and Zipp 1996). Contrastingly, Republican female candidates give mixed voting cues. The identity associated with gender competes with that associated with party affiliation as a cue for voting behavior (ibid.). Voters must deal with conflicting cues particularly concerning social issues when evaluating Republican female candidates. Consequently, the Democratic Party is both more likely to appeal to as well as actually recruit female candidates (Biersack and Herrnson 1994). According to Burrell (1994), women could be more likely to run as Democrats for several reasons. She suggests that women might run as Democrats because: they have a greater likelihood of winning; there are more Democratic female state legislators; there are more Democratic open seats; and Democratic party culture is more receptive to women as candidates than Republican party culture.

In the interview data for this analysis, Members and their staff discussed their personal decisions to run for congressional office, the nature of their districts, and the relative difficulty of their campaigns. Interviews with party elites echoed these themes and also shed light on the recruitment process. All of the respondents commented on the difficulty Republican women have in securing congressional seats. The following discussion highlights the findings from these interviews and illustrates the unique electoral circumstances faced by women in Congress.

The Decision to Run

One of the clearest partisan patterns I observed while conducting interviews with Members and their staff concerned legislators' decisions to run for Congress. While Democratic Members largely came from backgrounds in social work or education, Republican Members largely came from political or business backgrounds or had politically active families. Though gender theory suggests that women are more likely than men to be motivated to run for office because of some specific issue (Fox 1997), the data for this research suggest that this finding is an artifact of partisanship rather than gender. The Democratic Party advocates the traditional "women's issues" that typically motivate and prioritize women's political involvement (Thomas 1994; Conway, Steuernagel, and Ahern 1997). While Democrats were motivated to run for congressional office by issues or issue-relevant professional backgrounds, Republicans were motivated by previous political experience and a driving political philosophy. See table 2.1 for a presentation of female Members' routes to congressional office.

Democrats
For Democratic Members, issues or professional backgrounds were the driving force behind their decision to run. Democratic Members and staff noted issues as the impetus for the decision to run. Take, for example, Rep. Carolyn McCarthy (D-NY), motivated to run for Congress on the issue of gun control by the death of her husband and son due to a shooting. Interestingly, the Democratic Members who did mention issues were predominantly African American. A staff for one such male Member reflected:

> (Member X's) interest in running for office did not stem from a political family background. He was the first in his family to be elected to Congress in (state X), just as he was the first to be elected to the federal bench. What interested him was where he grew up. He was a civil rights leader. As an attorney, he was involved in desegregation.

Similarly, a staff for another senior black Democratic male Member noted that it was the Member's involvement in the civil rights movement that motivated his political career. He was part of the historic march that was the catalyst of the Voting Rights Act.

Some Democratic women get involved in congressional politics because of their profession. One staff remarked that her Member "was a former substitute teacher that gained political experience before running for Congress." Still another noted that his boss was a former nurse who "has a heart for helping people." They work in professions directly associated with

Table 2.1 Routes to office of women serving in the house during the 107th Congress

	Democratic women	Republican women
State Representative or Senator	25 (56.82%)	9 (50%)
City Council Member	10 (22.73%)	1 (5.56%)
County Commissioner or Supervisor	6 (13.64%)	1 (5.56%)
Mayor	2 (4.55%)	2 (11.11%)
Party Activist	4 (9.09%)	1 (5.56%)
School/University Board Member	4 (9.09%)	2 (11.11%)
Educator	16 (36.36%)	7 (38.89%)
Nurse/Physician	4 (9.09%)	0 (0.00%)
Businesswoman	4 (9.09%)	7 (38.89 %)
Attorney/Judge	6 (13.64%)	3 (16.67%)
Advocate/Lobbyist	3 (6.82%)	2 (11.11%)
Congressional Staff	4 (9.09%)	0 (0.00%)
White House Staff	3 (6.82%)	0 (0.00%)
Administrator	2 (4.55%)	2 (11.11%)
Civil Servant	2 (4.55%)	1 (5.56%)
Widow	1 (2.27%)	2 (11.11%)
Political Family Background	5 (11.36%)	6 (33.33%)
Valid *N*	42	18

Source: Data provided by the Center for American Women and Politics (CAWP), National Information Bank on Women in Public Office, Eagleton Institute of Politics, Rutgers University (2002).

social issues traditionally considered women's issues, such as education and healthcare.

Yet some in Democratic leadership are concerned about the effects that women running on issues have for reaching out to women nationally. A senior staffer in a Democratic leadership office noted:

> When a woman Democrat says anything about guns, the public perceives her to be extreme. As Democrats, we have not done a good enough job at the local level to identify, nurture, and support female candidates in order for them to prove credible. The Republicans have done a better job at that. Take this scenario for example. A small business person at a chamber of commerce meeting considers herself a Republican. She considers herself pro-choice and for equal pay. Her social circle and networking however is Republican. This identification becomes how she gets along, but she doesn't realize that Republicans don't support the programs she believes in. We count on women candidates figuring that out on their own. . . .

Because women make up 50 percent of the voting population, female candidates are better able to appeal to all districts than minority candidates and thus have enjoyed quicker advancement to higher levels of politics. Consequently, this senior Democratic staff person reiterated the importance of reaching out to more women by:

> having our female Members articulate other messages. We need new African American women like Juanita Millender-McDonald. We need Carolyn McCarthy on mainstream issues rather than guns. We need women to take credit for their non-traditional stances, like Jane Harman who is pro-defense. Ellen Tauscher, a fiscal conservative, needs to be out there.

Republicans

For Republicans, the pattern was very different. Republican women by and large seemed motivated to run for Congress by political backgrounds— and importantly, their own political backgrounds. A senior staffer in a Republican leadership office noted that just twenty years ago,

> very few (Republican) women were elected on their own. All of them were widows. They left service in the 80's, and a new breed started in the 90's. The others worked hard, but they were brought here by their husbands.

In an examination of the congressional careers of sixty-six women elected to the House between 1917 and 1970, Bullock and Heys (1972) found that nearly a majority of them (47%) were widows who filled their late husbands' seats. According to the leadership of the National Federation of Republican Women, several convergent factors have been at work to encourage female Republicans to run independently:

> In the early 90's, at the national level, we began looking to women who had been elected before at other levels of government. First and foremost, these women know the demands of holding elective office; they are well versed in issues; they have proven they can win, and that they can raise money. Women weren't stepping up as much. Then 1992, the "Year of the Woman," and we didn't do that well. This is when women in the party realized that it took more than just being a woman. People want more than a "woman's perspective." All issues are issues for all of us. More became willing to step up and run, and realized that voters want more than women's issues. We gained the majority in 1994, and for the first time had women in leadership positions in the House. We put the spotlight on them; they were good role models. Then we started providing campaign management schools, and there was also the natural progression of the increase in local women office-holders. We are on the executive committee of the RNC. There has been a real effort at the national level with Anne Wagner (Vice Chair of the RNC).

Nearly 85 percent (11 out of 13) of the congressional aides to female Republican Members interviewed commented on the Representative's political or legislative qualifications for elective office. Some noted the political family background of the Member. One staff for a Republican female Member explained that she "came from a political family. Her father was a congressman and governor. Given that her district is a swing district, the party definitely had interest in her long before the election." Another staff for a female Republican Member noted "her Dad was the executive director of the RNC. She felt the need to carry on the family name. There is a 16-year history of holding the seat. There was a whole host of party recruiters convincing her to run."

Others talked about the political experience of the Member that qualified her to run for Congress. One staff for a Republican female Member, when asked what interested her Member in running for Congress, noted: "She was the (X) state party chair for 12 years. She worked on Goldwater's campaign. She is a huge Reaganite and a fiscal conservative. She believes we ought to get government out of personal issues, we ought to make government smaller." Another stated that her Republican female Member "had previous political experience and likes public service. When (Member X) retired, the local GOP knew her." One of the most interesting stories concerning the decision to run involved a more senior female Republican Member. Her staff recounted the early days of the Member's political career:

> She had previous political experience. She was on the school board, and ran her area for (Candidate X's) gubernatorial campaign. There were a number of party activists and leadership at the local and regional level that urged her to take on the incumbent for her congressional district. She attended the NRCC's campaign school on how to run and win in the mid 1980's—they called it "charm school." In fact, G. W. (Bush) named her "Charm-School (first-name of Member X)."

While the vast majority of women elected to represent Republican districts come from political families or backgrounds, some do not. Some expressed the hardships they faced getting the endorsement of the party given their background outside of political life. One staff for a Republican female Member noted that she responded to a "grassroots public outcry. She was number one in real estate. The party came on late once they realized she was going to win." Still others who had political experience recounted difficulty in gaining the party endorsement. One staff remarked:

> (Member X) had previous political experience. . . . She was recruited, but not everyone in the party agreed on who the candidate should be. It was a split endorsement. The key issue was abortion. In the primary, she ran against a

very conservative Republican. She walked the fence enough to get elected. . . . She comes from an urban area with suburbs and a college and some rural areas that are Midwest moderate. She's a good balance. She receives 70% of the vote now. Guns and abortion are two issues in which she's out of sync with conservative Republicans.

For some, the marginality of the district combined with previous political experience worked to their advantage in gaining the party endorsement. One staff for a Republican female Member said:

She's a grassroots campaigner. She had no political connections or family money. She was the only Republican in the area down the board. But she understands the legislative process; she has a legal background. She has ten years experience as a state legislator, and that definitely impacts business here.

One staff for an electorally focused Republican female Member offered rich insight into the problem Republican women face in gaining the party's endorsement. She suggested that it is not necessarily the lack of qualified female candidates, but rather the lack of consideration given to them by male party elites. She stated:

Men (in the local party organization) will sit around and talk about candidates. Whenever talking about civic or community service positions they will ask women to serve, but when talking about political office, they don't. Women are used to being asked. When they aren't asked, they tend to not feel qualified or adequate. We (women) have to shift the paradigm and just run.

For many, the contours of the district determine the electoral fate of the Member. When asked how the party generally handles recruitment, a high-ranking Republican leadership staffer noted:

The party actively recruits challengers. It is a function of the RNC and NRCC. . . . We work with the representatives already in the state for recommendations. Then we look at the make-up of districts for racial diversity, democratic registration, and union membership. We go district-by-district and try to find candidates early so that we can get grassroots mobilization and fundraising early on. Then we send in the leadership team to raise the profile of the candidate and raise money. It's hard to recruit candidates unless there is lots of money to back them. It's even hard with money because of all the media scrutiny and family scrutiny.

A director at the NRCC contended that the party's handling of recruitment depends on the seat. He observed: "If the seat is one we can hold, then we're pretty much hands off. It it's competitive, we then try to promote the candidate. We try to stay neutral, but at times we help to find a strong candidate if one has not already been identified."

In discussing the criteria involved in the recruitment of female candidates, he remarked:

> The most important category is "electability." If the candidate is a state representative from the corner of a district and is up against a state senator, then the candidate has low electability. These criteria include things like ideological orientation and compatibility with the district.

When asked what characteristics the party looks for in female recruits, a director in a Republican leadership office stated: "Being a woman—that's what they look for." She elaborated that "it's always tricky; it depends on the district." When pushed on specific criteria such as confidence, ambition, attractiveness, and education, she noted: "They like ambition the least. Male party leaders are the ones doing the recruiting. What they think is appealing to the public is a woman who's not too aggressive." Similarly, the director from the NRCC noted that "women can be too aggressive," but he also noted "they can also be too soft." He elaborated:

> It's hard to just check off a box. If everybody says "she's a bitch," but she's majority leader, they'll say "she gets stuff done." If they have a record of getting stuff done, they can be hard core and it not work against them. Some might even view it as a good quality. We look to the candidate and tell her to use it to her advantage—use her qualities to her advantage.

A majority of the Republican party elites I interviewed (five of eight) noted that the family background of female candidates is becoming increasingly important in the recruitment process. The NRCC director stated:

> A woman's family background allows her credibility on issues, such as: family issues, education issues, social issues, and abortion. . . . Female candidates discuss family background more than men because when females have children and aren't in the workforce, they have to use that time to their advantage and integrate it into their qualifications as work experience or a positive quality. You wouldn't buy it if a man used it as experience, but it is bought from women. They are thought of as care givers. There's no question that women are still breaking barriers. The first thing that jumps out with female recruits is what they've done to qualify them for office. Men can just say, 'I believe in . . . and that's why I'm running.'

In fact, six (33%) of the Republican women in office in the 106th Congress came from political families, according to the Center for American Women in Politics (CAWP). Political family background as well as the other routes to office was coded from the biographical sketches provided by the CAWP (2002). If the sketch mentioned the political associations of the female Member's family in any way, that Member was coded as having a political family background. In terms of the interview data, the definition of family background was left to the discretion of the party elites. Family background along with the ability to raise campaign funds seem to be the most important criteria involved in the party's perception of female candidates. As another Republican leadership staffer commented: "The party looks for money. If a challenger is individually wealthy, she is automatically a candidate. The ability to raise money is highly attractive."

District Marginality

Several district-level factors combine to form electoral pressures on a Member. Marginality is a concept that is often used to describe the extent to which a congressional seat is competitive. It refers to a number of contexts. First, a seat is considered marginal if the general ideology of the district is more moderate than the party holding the seat. Secondly, a seat is considered marginal if the vote returns for the Member are barely a majority. According to Mayhew (1974), a Member represents a marginal seat if he or she captures less than 55 percent of the vote. This standard, however, is not sufficient for measuring marginality in the present context (Jacobson 1987). According to Jacobson (1987):

> Electoral data show that House incumbents are no safer now than they were in the 1950s, the marginals properly defined have not vanished; the swing ration has diminished little, if at all; and competition for House seats held by incumbents has not declined. Vote margins increased without adding to incumbent security, diminishing competition, or dampening swings. (126)

This research suggests that marginality still influences Member behavior, but that the standard for marginality has changed. Elections are more volatile, so Members are unsafe at wider margins than in decades past. Consequently, the measure used for this analysis is 60 percent. Members who receive 60 percent of the vote or more are defined as safe; Members who receive less than 60 percent of the vote are defined as marginal. Multiple measures of marginality were tested in developing the analysis for this chapter as well as the sections of the project that follows. Marginality defined as 55 percent, 60 percent, and 65 percent produced generally the same results. For the purpose of this project, the 60 percent measure was incorporated because not only is it supported by the literature, but it also provided enough cases in the marginal as well as the secure category to provide meaningful interpretation.

It is important for us to consider district marginality when examining women's political participation because marginality can have a significant impact on legislative behavior. Recent rational choice theory suggests that Members in safe seats with wide electoral margins enjoy more "discretion" than Members in competitive districts (Parker 1992). In other words, they have more freedom to pursue their own policy goals or higher inter- or intra-institutional offices.

Several factors are thought to lead to electoral competition or marginality. In particular, district heterogeneity or diversity is thought to be associated with marginality (Froman 1963; Fiorina 1974; Koetzle 1998). The district diversity thesis suggests that "members from diverse districts are likely to experience more electoral competition than other members from relatively less diverse districts" (Koetzle 1998, 562). Analyses examining this association, however, have produced mixed results (see Bond 1983, 1985).

Proponents of the diversity thesis point to the disparate constituencies to which the American political parties appeal. Republicans typically represent whites, higher income populations, white-collar workers, Protestants, and suburban voters. Democrats, on the other hand, typically represent blacks and other minority populations, lower income populations, blue-collar workers, and urban voters (Berelson, Lazarsfeld, and McPhee 1954; Campbell, Miller, Converse, and Stokes 1960; Froman 1963; Levy and Kramer 1976; Wolfinger and Rosenstone 1980; Huckfeldt and Kohfled 1989; Aistrup 1996; Miller and Stokes 1996). In diverse districts, or districts that are a mix of these two conglomerations, Koetzel suggests:

> we might expect the distribution of opinion to be more centered than in homogeneous districts. In this situation, each party is better able to field candidates ideologically attractive to a significant portion of the constituency. This, in turn, leads to relatively higher levels of electoral competition. (562)

In my interviews, clear patterns developed regarding the electoral constraints female Members face due to marginality. There are marginal seats on both sides of the aisle. A staff for a Democratic female Member noted the electoral constraints faced by the Member.

> She's in a Republican district, so she doesn't vote along party lines all the time. Take for example the tax cut; she personally disagreed, but it was in the district's interest. She would follow the party line more if she was in a Democratic district. She often doesn't have a choice on what or how to vote if she wants to retain her seat.

Female Republican Members and their staff, however, provided the majority of the comments regarding marginality. A few female Republican Members specifically drew attention to their electoral situation that constrained their participation more than their co-partisan male colleagues.

These Members and staff pointed to the ideological marginality of the district as a constraint on legislative behavior. More specifically, social issues seemed to pose problems for Members' vote decisions. Out of the thirteen female Republican offices interviewed, ten were characterized as representing marginal or socially moderate districts by the staff and/or Member. A staff for one Republican female Member noted that she:

> struggles more with social issues because of her district. It is fiscally conservative. Thankfully, on her committee, she doesn't have to deal with the "prickly issues," like abortion and gun control, because the district is divided. It has both rural and urban areas. Both [she] (the Member) and Gore took the district by 65%.

This comment further serves to highlight the volatility of elections and the idea that Members perceive themselves as marginal even when receiving a greater percentage of the vote than traditionally considered by the political science literature as marginal.

Another staff for a Republican female Member noted that she comes from a "very depressed state." Consequently, her top three legislative priorities are: "economic development, prescription drug coverage, and infrastructure." He later commented that "all her legislative priorities are district driven."

Some noted that these constraints posed personal ideological problems for the Member. One staff for a Republican female Member noted that she comes from a "Democratic district," elaborating that, "She's socially conservative (pro-life and pro-gun), but she has to toe the line on unions for example. She sees tax cuts as a route to job creation to address the needs of her district which is economically-depressed."

These electoral constraints do not simply condition the Member's vote; they also structure their time and attention. A staff for a female Republican Member noted:

> She brings back more money than we ever thought possible to the district. She has an intonation for what people want to hear. She wants to be involved in everything because it's her neck that's on the line. She is involved in the direct mail, the franked mail. She rewrote the entire franked mail education piece last year. She's incredibly hands on; she's very in touch with what's going on in the office. She emphasizes her soft side. It's two-to-one registered Democrats in the district. She emphasizes education, seniors, healthcare; she

doesn't talk about tax cuts in the district. She's not putting out legislative proposals right now. It was no legislation, just appropriations pieces up until ergonomics—that was the first substantive policy issue that we worked on. She's very election-focused. She had three ads against her last election cycle by June.

Not only do female Republican Members see their districts as requiring more attention because of issues, they also understand their personal ambition constrained by electoral demands. One staff for a female Republican Member noted:

> She couldn't ever run for leadership because she's too busy securing her own race. But she would have been great (in leadership) because none of them are from vulnerable districts. She anticipates the train or the storm and would be a good spot check. If something is going to happen, she's the first to hear the rumbling.

The additional attention necessary for the district also poses time constraints in Washington. Several Members noted that because they were from marginal districts they were required to participate in more political activities sponsored by the National Republican Campaign Committee. In return for political support, they were expected to participate in party meetings and events. The NRCC director explained:

> 20% of the organizational meetings involve the full conference; 40% of meetings include active folks in politics who want to be involved in the team; and the other 40% of meetings are attended by people who have to be involved and active because they need to be reelected and they're trying to score points.

One staff for a Republican female Member noted that his Member is a "targeted Member" meaning that she is in a marginal district and receives great attention by the NRCC. For this reason, she regularly attends the NRCC meetings and fundraisers (averaging twice a month). Another staff for a Republican female Member explained that her district is a "swing district." She is also considered a "targeted member." He further explained:

> She is on the 'ROMP list' or the 'Retain Our Majority Party' list. This list is composed of seven to ten of the most vulnerable Members. The NRCC has events with this group. They are given the very best treatment. She is a very valuable Member in a competitive district, so she is top on the list.

He further suggested that the marginality of her district has consequences for her party activity, stating: "It's a tough position to be in. She is a freshman in a vulnerable seat. She is going to be given some leeway, but we have to dissent at the right time."

Nevertheless, these Republican women do serve a vital function in the party. As one staff remarked:

> 90% of the time, she votes Republican. She's a great fundraiser, and she's a great communicator when properly focused. And she holds a seat that would never hold a man. She appeals to soccer moms. She comes from a large family and talks about policy in the context of her family.

In this short bit of dialogue, this staffer articulates the function of women within the party. These women add a new face to the Republican Party. They communicate the message in a distinctive way that appeals to a different, more liberal audience. They do not always vote with the party, but can be counted on most of the time. And most importantly, they secure seats that otherwise would be unattainable by Republicans. The ability of Republican women to communicate to a different, more feminine audience is valued not just by the female legislators themselves, but also by their party leadership. As one senior Republican leadership staff noted:

> Their contribution is that they understand better than men family concerns and the challenges of raising a family. That's why they're biased towards those types of issues (e.g. education and healthcare). Men don't own the problem. The women understand what 50% of voters go through in trying to raise a family. Even Democratic men are biased towards numbers (e.g. taxes and defense). The women bring a sense of community, even the conservative women like Barbara Cubin understand that. The conservative men just don't get it.

It appears that the evaluations expressed by staff and Members regarding electoral constraints are not too far fetched. Whichever way we define marginality, female Republican Members generally represent more marginal districts than their co-partisan male colleagues (see table 2.2).

Overall, female Republican Members win their elections by narrower margins than male Republican Members. Both before and after the Republican take-over of Congress, Republican women represented more marginal districts than men. The only exception to this generalization is in the 105th Congress, or the election of 1996. In this year, Republican men held a slightly lower average rate of electoral return than Republican women. Perhaps this is attributable to the public backlash to the excesses of Gingrich control during the first hundred days of the 104th Congress (Ornstein and Schenkenberg 1995). It is also possible that this anomaly reflects the marginality of the large freshmen class of 1994 who had not yet

Table 2.2 Electoral returns across Congresses by party and sex

		103rd	104th	105th	106th	107th
Republican men	Mean	62.65%	67.57%	64.02%	70.25%	66.79%
	s.d.	(11.80)	(14.64)	(11.00)	(14.78)	(11.52)
	N	164	214	211	205	205
	% Secure	55.5%	67.8%	63.5%	75.1%	69.8%
	N	91	145	134	154	143
	% Marginal	44.5%	32.2%	36.5%	24.9%	30.2%
	N	73	69	77	51	62
Republican women	Mean	58.92%	65.82%	64.59%	64.59%	62.89%
	s.d.	(9.76)	(15.82)	(16.02)	(14.22)	(11.30)
	N	12	17	17	17	18
	% Secure	41.7%	58.8%	47.1%	70.6%	61.1%
	N	5	10	8	12	11
	% Marginal	58.3%	41.2%	52.9%	29.4%	38.9%
	N	7	7	9	5	7
Democratic men	Mean	64.28%	63.75%	64.15%	71.42%	71.33%
	s.d.	(11.50)	(12.72)	(12.37)	(14.86)	(13.75)
	N	223	173	168	173	170
	% Secure	59.6%	54.3%	58.9%	71.7%	76.5%
	N	133	94	99	124	130
	% Marginal	40.4%	45.7%	41.1%	28.3%	23.5%
	N	90	79	69	49	40
Democratic women	Mean	64.11%	66.80%	65.84%	70.15%	69.52%
	s.d.	(12.29)	(12.91)	(12.55)	(13.03)	(13.17)
	N	35	30	38	39	42
	% Secure	54.3%	63.3%	63.2%	71.8%	73.8%
	N	19	19	24	28	31
	% Marginal	45.7%	36.7%	36.8%	28.2%	26.2%
	N	16	11	14	11	11

Standard deviations are presented in parentheses and represented by s.d. The valid N represents the number in the category. The figure indicating % secure represents the percentage of Members in that category receiving at least 60% of the vote. Conversely, the figure indicating % marginal represents the percentage of Members in that category receiving less than 60% of the vote.

established an incumbency advantage. The years surrounding the Republican Revolution are considered to be unstable years, however, and thus we should be careful to draw conclusions based on data from these years.

It is important to note nonetheless that during years of partisan stability the pattern is even more pronounced. In 1992, Republican women had the lowest average vote return of any category of Members. At 58.92 percent, they were lower than Republican men (62.65%), Democratic men (64.28%), and Democratic women (64.11%). Similarly, in 1998, Republican women repeated the pattern. With 64.59 percent, they enjoyed markedly higher average returns, but still were lower than Republican men (70.25%), Democratic men (71.42%), and Democratic women (70.15%). Also of note is the fact that Democratic women as a group enjoy larger electoral margins than Republican women in every congress in the sample.

Dichotomizing the electoral vote return variable provides us with a basic measure of security. To construct this variable, I coded safe Members as those Members receiving 60 percent or more of the vote, and unsafe Members as those Members receiving less than 60 percent of the vote. Table 2.3 provides the percentages of Members defined as safe and unsafe by party and gender. Similarly, figure 2.1 provides a visual depiction of Member marginality across congresses by party and gender. Generally, Members of the U.S. House of Representatives since the 103rd Congress have become more and more electorally safe. Across all categories, there is a general trend toward electoral security. This figure also clearly demonstrates that Republican women have the largest percentage of marginal Members of any group. Except for the 104th Congress when a slightly larger percentage of

Table 2.3 Average district presidential return across Congresses by party and sex

	103rd	104th	105th	106th	107th
Republican men	35.92%	36.76%	42.55%	42.36%	55.93%
	(6.35)	(6.13)	(6.57)	(6.49)	(7.94)
	164	214	211	205	205
Republican women	37.67%	36.71%	45.12%	44.41%	52.22%
	(5.85)	(5.72)	(6.25)	(6.02)	(7.99)
	12	17	17	17	18
Democratic men	48.17%	50.85%	58.04%	57.64%	39.24%
	(12.41)	(12.67)	(12.79)	(12.58)	(13.96)
	223	173	167	173	170
Democratic women	55.00%	57.47%	61.68%	62.49%	31.07%
	(12.90)	(12.14)	(12.30)	(12.23)	(11.58)
	35	30	38	39	42

Note: Standard deviations in parentheses with valid *N* present below.

The presidential vote in the district is coded as the percent of the vote that went to the winning party. In the case of the 106th Congress (1999–2000), it would be the percentage of the vote that went to Democratic winner, President Clinton, in the 1996 presidential election. In the case of the 107th Congress (2001–2002), it would be the percent of the vote that went to Republican winner, President George W. Bush, in the 2000 presidential election. For this reason, the pattern reverses from the 106th to the 107th Congresses.

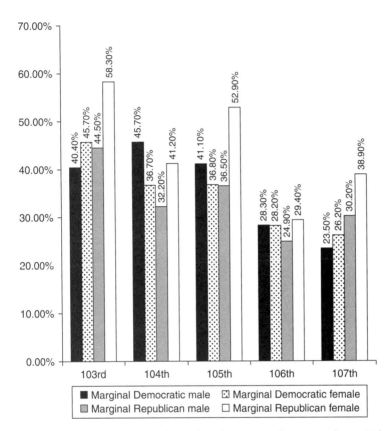

Figure 2.1 Percent of marginal members by party and sex: 103rd to 107th Congresses

Democratic men than Republican women were electorally marginal, this figure provides further evidence to suggest that Republican women suffer from greater electoral marginality than any other group. Further, on average the largest partisan gap in electoral security is between Republican men and Republican women. In other words, since the change of partisan control in the 104th Congress, Republican men as a group are the most electorally secure Members of Congress and Republican women are generally the least electorally secure Members of Congress.

Drawing from the interview data, it would seem that one of the primary differences between the districts represented by Republican men and Republican women is general ideology. Members and their staff suggested that female Republican Members represent districts that are on average more moderate than those represented by male Republican Members. Table 2.3 presents the average district presidential returns broken down by gender and partisanship of the Member. Districts represented by female Republican Members generally yielded higher returns for President Clinton in both 1992 and 1996, and lower returns for President George W. Bush, than districts represented by male Republican Members. In every congress except the 104th (in which the vote was basically even) "the vote for the Republican presidential candidate was higher" in Republican men's than women's districts. This measure of district ideology supports the notion that female Republicans do represent more marginal or moderate districts than male Republicans. In 1992, the average vote return for Clinton was 37.67 percent in districts represented by Republican women; it was 35.92 percent in districts represented by Republican men. Similarly, in 1996, the average presidential return was 45.12 percent in female Republican districts, and 42.55 percent in male Republican districts. In 2000, this trend continued with the vote return for George W. Bush averaging 55.93 percent in Republican men's districts and 52.22 percent in Republican women's districts.

Conversely, Democratic women represent districts with much higher average presidential vote returns than Democratic men. In 1992, the average vote return for Clinton was 55 percent in districts represented by Democratic women; it was 48.17 percent in districts represented by Democratic men. In 1996, the pattern was the same. The average presidential return was 61.68 percent in female Democratic districts, and 58.04 percent in male Democratic districts. In every congress, the GOP vote was substantially smaller in Democratic women's than Democratic men's districts. In 2000, in fact, the vote return for George W. Bush averaged 39.24 percent in Democratic men's districts and 31.07 percent in Democratic women's districts.

Connecting the Dots—From Electoral Behavior to Voting Behavior

Although voting behavior is given a much more thorough treatment in chapter 3 of the analysis, for the purposes of this presentation, it is helpful to briefly "connect the dots" between Members' electoral behavior and their general voting behavior. I employ the vote scaling techniques developed by Poole and Rosenthal (1985, 1991, 1997). These DW-NOMINATE scores were downloaded from Keith Poole's data archive on the web at: http://voteview.uh.edu/default_nomdata.htm and are recorded for the

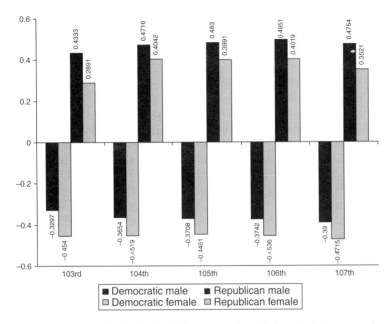

Figure 2.2   Mean DW-NOMINATE scores for the 103rd to 107th Congresses by sex and partisanship

103rd through 107th Congresses. DW-NOMINATE scores are useful in that they can be compared across congresses. DW-NOMINATE scores provide a single measure of ideology, bounded between −1 and +1 with conservatism increasing in a positive direction on a single left–right continuum. It is created from collapsing all legislative roll call votes into a single score reflecting a Member's overall ideology. One major benefit of using this measure is that scores can be compared across congresses thus allowing us to draw conclusions from data spanning the 103rd through the 107th Congresses.

Figure 2.2 illustrates mean differences between male and female voting behavior from the 103rd Congress to the 107th Congress given partisanship. While this is simply a graph of average DW-NOMINATE scores, it serves to illustrate the ever-growing partisan polarization among Members of Congress. Across all congresses, women are more liberal than their male partisan colleagues. However, there is a clearly delineated pattern of partisan voting among both men and women. Female Republicans are much more conservative than male or female Democrats. Conversely, female Democrats are much more liberal than male or female Republicans.

To test whether the differences in means between the independent populations (Democratic males and Democratic females, and Republican males and Republican females) were significant, two tests were used: Levene's test for equality of variances and independent sample t tests (assuming normal distributions) and Mann–Whitney and Kolmogorov–Smirnov tests (assuming nonparametric distributions). Since the 104th Congress, the differences in means have been more pronounced between Democratic males and females than between Republican males and females.

In the aftermath of the Republican takeover of Congress, the gap between Republican male and female Members narrowed for some time. Till the 107th Congress, Republican women appeared to be growing more and more conservative in their voting behavior. This is further significant given that the number of Republican women increased by a third from the 103rd Congress to the 107th Congress (from 12 to 18). In the 107th Congress, however, the gap between the ideological voting behavior of Republican women and men more closely mirrored that of the 103rd Congress. Democratic women, on the other hand, stayed relatively ideologically stable across congresses. While Democratic men became a little more conservative overall, this difference was minimal.

The argument of this chapter is that partisanship structures women's behavior in the Congress. We examined how the electoral circumstance of female Members is shaped by their partisanship. We found that Republican women represent more moderate districts, and must devote additional resources to electoral concerns in order to secure their seats. This finding raises an important question concerning women's voting behavior given their electoral security. How does electoral security influence women's voting behavior? Are electorally marginal women more likely to vote with their district than their party? Should we expect Republican women to illustrate more liberal voting behavior when they are electorally marginal?

Figure 2.3 illustrates average Member DW-NOMINATE scores by party, gender, and electoral security. This figure demonstrates a clear difference in voting behavior based on electoral security. There is a consistent, discernable difference in the voting behavior of marginal versus secure Members. For Democrats, this difference is in the expected direction. We would expect more marginal Democratic Members to represent more moderate districts and thus vote more conservatively than their colleagues. Marginal Democratic women voted an average of 0.1075 points more conservatively than secure Democratic women. Similarly, there was a 0.725 difference in the voting behavior of secure and marginal Democratic men, with marginal men voting more conservatively than electorally safe men.

Interestingly, the pattern is in the opposite direction for Republicans. While we would expect marginal Republican Members to represent more

45

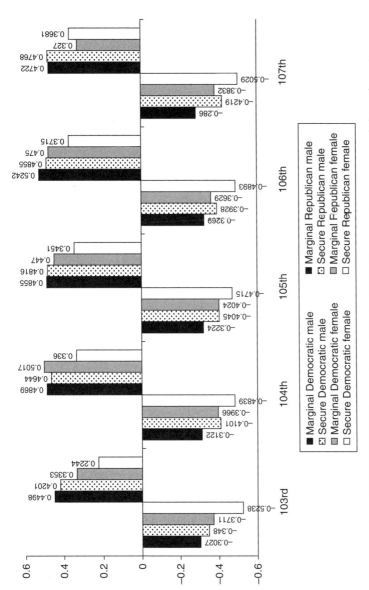

Figure 2.3 Mean DW-NOMINATE scores for the 103rd to 107th Congresses by party, sex, and electoral security

moderate districts and thus vote more liberally than their colleagues, this is not the case. Although the mean difference is slight, marginal Republican men voted on average 0.002 points more conservatively than secure Republican men in every congress except the 107th. Similarly, but more significantly, marginal Republican women voted on average 0.12 points more conservatively than secure Republican women in every congress except the 107th. The 107th Congress marks the first time across years that safe Republicans voted more conservatively than marginal Republicans. Perhaps this anomaly is due to more conservative Members elected in the 104th Congress under the leadership of Newt Gingrich gaining seniority and enjoying the increased electoral security of incumbency.

To test whether the differences in means between the independent populations (marginal and secure Democratic males; marginal and secure Democratic females; marginal and secure Republican males; and marginal and secure Republican females) were significant, two tests were used: Levene's test for equality of variances and independent sample t tests (assuming normal distributions) and Mann–Whitney and Kolmogorov–Smirnov tests (assuming nonparametric distributions). The results indicated significant differences in means for Democrats, and significant differences in distributions for Republicans. Since the 104th Congress, the differences in means have been more pronounced between secure and marginal Democrats, but the differences in distribution have been more pronounced between secure and marginal Republicans. This suggests that Democratic mean ideology scores are significantly associated with electoral security (marginal Members voting more moderately than secure Members). While Republican mean ideology scores are not significantly associated with electoral security, the distributions between secure and marginal Members are significantly different. In other words, the range for electorally secure Republican Members is much more limited than it is for electorally marginal Republican Members.

What can we conclude from these findings? This pattern further illustrates differences in the cultures of the Republican and Democratic parties. Republican Members respond to electoral marginality by securing their partisan base through more conservative voting. They act like Republicans. This also ensures them further support from the national party organization. Democratic Members, on the other hand, attempt to expand their base through more moderate voting. They respond to diverse constituent pressures. Doing so does not affect their support from the national party organization that fosters constituent responsiveness and ideological diversity.

It appears that, in general, women are more attuned to electoral marginality than men. Also, based on average ideological voting behavior, Democratic Members seem more reactive than Republican Members to electoral vulnerabilities. They seem more responsive to constituent pressures.

Conclusion and Implications

Partisanship is perpetually the strongest predictor of legislative behavior. Nevertheless, in recent decades, rational choice theory has refocused attention on the electoral and political goals of individual Members as explanations of voting behavior. Members are treated as "single-minded seekers of reelection" (Mayhew 1974). Consequently, since the initial work of Mayhew (1974), Fiorina (1977), and Fenno (1978), congressional theory has addressed the electoral incentive by including district-level indicators in models of legislative behavior. Recent rational choice theory further suggests the importance of electoral margins in predicting Members' voting behavior. Members in safe seats with wide electoral margins enjoy more "discretion" than Members in competitive districts (Parker 1992).

The female Members and staff interviewed for this analysis suggest that women do face unique electoral pressures, and that these pressures are contingent upon partisanship. While Democratic women on average represent more liberal districts than their male colleagues, Republican women represent more moderate districts than their male colleagues. In addition, these Republican women represent more electorally marginal seats than any of their other colleagues.

This unique district context shapes Republican women's participation within the institution in important ways. First, they must spend more of their time and effort on district issues. Second, their electoral situation contours their involvement in the national party apparatus. Republican women do not enjoy the time necessary to pursue leadership positions. They also do not have the luxury of disregarding political fundraising activities. The party, nonetheless, does value them. Republican women secure congressional seats that might not otherwise be included in the Republican camp. They do, however, find themselves operating in a party culture that values ideological homogeneity and partisan loyalty. While the party does grant them some discretion to vote on behalf of their districts, they must break rank strategically in order to avoid losing favor with party leadership.

Democratic women, on the other hand, enjoy substantial discretion due to their electoral security. It should be noted, however, that the ideological homogeneity and issue-driven political careers of senior female Democratic Members hold national consequences for the party. A senior staff person in Democratic leadership noted that in the contemporary context "while female candidates are viewed as more trustworthy and more honest," they are also seen as "more liberal."

This public stereotype is reinforced by the seniority system that dominates the culture of the Democratic Party. According to this same staff person:

> People assume that they (female Democratic Members) are militantly pro-choice and anti-defense. That's just not true. Women represent districts that hold those views. In particular, senior women from more liberal districts keep our new moderate women from getting more exposure. Women in the party should be used more and a little differently. We should send a counter-intuitive message. We shouldn't have women articulate our most liberal positions. Female Democrats support the more liberal, more urban positions, but it's less who they are than who they represent. We have women minority members in the Democratic Party; there aren't any on the Republican side. It's impressive that female Members are elected by minorities in minority districts. Their extreme liberal positions, however, are less reflective of male and female differences than they are of minority constituency interests. And those are the constituencies who are almost always going to vote for them.

From this discussion, it appears that the electoral connection is important to women's legislative behavior. Because electoral politics are structured by political parties, we might expect partisanship to influence the electoral pressures faced by Members. In fact, it does influence women's political participation in significant and meaningful ways. For Democratic women, the general demographics and ideology of the district grant the discretion to participate positively in party politics. For Republican women, district characteristics and pressures inhibit certain forms of partisan involvement and demand others. Chapter 3 more thoroughly examines the institutional connection. How do electoral pressures translate into the voting behavior of women within the context of partisanship? What district factors or Member characteristics are associated with ideological voting?

This analysis has important implications for women's participation in Congress. Partisanship plays a very real and significant role in contouring the legislative behavior of women. The first arena where this relationship is evident is the electoral arena. Party culture operates even at the level of electoral politics. From recruitment to electoral outcomes, parties shape congressional campaigns.

In terms of participation, Democratic women are relatively free to pursue electoral security through constituent responsiveness. Republican women, on the other hand, must balance partisan loyalty with district interests in order to ensure future electoral success. Republican women express frustration because of limitations created by electoral marginality. They are limited in the resources they can devote to partisan activities. They are restricted in the time and effort they can give to institutional pursuits.

Even if these findings were based on merely perceptual evidence, they still would hold significant implications for the participation of Republican women. But Republican women do face the most competitive elections that only serve to reaffirm their perceptions. Not only do women already face many obstacles to political participation that men do not face, but also, as Bledsoe and Herring (1990) suggest, political circumstance also influences their pursuit of higher office. They state:

> Compared to men, women are more likely to be influenced in making a bid for higher office by the strength of their current political position and their perception of their political vulnerability. Women who see themselves as electorally vulnerable are unlikely to try for higher office. (1990, 221)

In the end, we find discernable differences in the behavior of male and female Members, even when considering partisanship. Yet evaluating women's behavior outside the context of partisanship grossly misrepresents their participation. We also find discernable differences in Member behavior associated with electoral security. These findings, however, must be interpreted within the context of partisanship. Women are aware of their electoral vulnerability. Their voting behavior reflects their electoral circumstance. In the end, however, their voting behavior reflects the patterns of their respective parties. Electorally marginal Republican women vote like electorally marginal Republican men, and electorally marginal Democratic women vote like electorally marginal Democratic men.

Chapter 3

Do Women in Congress Vote Alike?

The Institutional Connection

I'm afraid you have come to the wrong place. I'm not going to be of much help to your study. You see, Jocelyn, I am an elected congresswoman. I was elected to represent all the views of my district. I don't ever look at issues as gender-oriented.

—Female Republican Member

Introduction

Traditionally, female Members of Congress have been thought to be more liberal than men. Although a few early studies of women's voting scores suggested this trend (Leader 1977; Welch 1985), the pattern has varied over time (see Vega and Firestone 1995). In the end, gender is only one factor in the complex matrix of Members' voting behavior. Many other factors, such as the Member's constituency interests, party affiliation, personal ideology, and ethnicity, are much stronger predictors of his or her voting behavior in Congress (Welch 1985; Vega and Firestone 1995; Schwindt 2000). For example, Swers (2002) states: "The influence of gender on a member's legislative behavior is highly dependent on his/her overall political ideology" (273).

In chapter 2, we explored Members' electoral connections examining the unique constituency pressures that women face. The partisan context of congressional districts is largely responsible for women's electoral circumstances. Members elected from the more liberal or conservative congressional districts enjoy greater electoral security, as well as the discretion and legislative freedom to pursue personal goals. For reasons not explored in this book, Democratic women represent some of the most liberal congressional districts in the country. District ideology and issue concerns mirror those of the left wing of the Democratic Party. Consequently, female Democratic Members enjoy electoral security and the additional discretion or legislative freedom that accompanies it.

Similarly, Republican women occupy congressional seats representing some of the most liberal districts within the fold of the Republican Party. District ideology and issue concerns do not reflect the ideology and priorities of the national party. These districts are some of the most vulnerable seats held by the Republican Party. Consequently, female Republican Members face more electoral vulnerability and less discretion than their male partisan colleagues. In other words, female Republican Members have significantly less freedom to pursue their personal goals and preferences than female Democratic Members.

Understanding the electoral circumstances of female legislators, we turn to the institutional connection. This chapter explores the voting behavior of women within the context of partisanship. Women are traditionally thought to be more ideologically alike and more liberal as a group, than men. We might expect this given the nature of the districts they by and large represent. The present analysis, however, demonstrates that women illustrate great diversity in their ideological leanings and this diversity is largely due to partisanship. In other words, Republican women illustrate more conservative voting patterns than Democratic women. While it is true that women generally are more liberal in their voting behavior than men, this generalization is accurate only in the context of partisanship. That is, female Republican Members exhibit more liberal voting behavior than male Republican Members, but they generally demonstrate more conservative voting behavior than male Democratic Members.

Several questions drive this chapter. First and foremost, does partisanship shape the voting behavior of female legislators in the House of Representatives? Second, if so, then is gender significantly associated with ideological voting behavior given the context of partisanship? In other words, do women vote differently from men of their same party? Is this relationship more significant when examining social issue voting, where women are traditionally thought to demonstrate more liberal ideological leanings?

In chapter 2, we discovered that women face a matrix of cross-pressures that are significantly structured by partisanship. We took these findings to be preliminary evidence of distinct party cultures. This chapter furthers this examination by applying it to Member behavior within the corridors of Congress. Here we examine the more general partisan contours of voting behavior. Are there identifiable differences between women Members of the two parties in terms of the institutional and constituency factors tradition-ally thought to be associated with Members' ideological voting behavior? Put another way, do all Members and specifically female Members respond differently to institutional as opposed to constituency pressures? And are these differences structured by partisanship?

Several theoretical questions bear on this discussion. If there are differ-ences between the ideological voting of the two parties, how do these dif-ferences affect representation? Do the different party cultures need different models of representation to explain their "style" of legislative behavior? And finally, what are the significant implications of different party cultures for the ideological behavior of female legislators?

Ideology as a Motivation for Political Behavior

Political ideology acts to guide, explain, and justify political action. Ideology "consist(s) of a set of ideas and principles relating to the purpose to pursue in political life and the methods to employ" (Van Dyke 1995, 1). The term "ideology" is "a symbol for the systems of political belief" (Miller and Shanks 1996, 121). Ideology provides structure, organization, and coherence of political thought. Both "cognitive matters—beliefs and patterns of atti-tudes—as well as affective matters—values and preferences . . . play a central role in facilitating understanding of the nature of one's world" (ibid.).

In order to mirror the diverse beliefs and values of voters, parties distin-guish themselves from each other on ideological grounds. "The party . . . is what it believes—its attitudes and perspectives, at all echelons" (Eldersveld 1964, 180). The party acts as a vital organ for developing stable issue pref-erences and positions by which members of Congress can orient themselves politically. It does so through the maintenance of a series of partisan-based committees such as the party caucus, policy committees, steering commit-tees, and informal groups (ibid.). Ippolito and Walker (1980) suggest:

> There are . . . major policy controversies that find many, if not all, congres-sional Democrats on one side and many, if not all, congressional Republicans

on the other. A concurrence of views characterizes each of the parties in
Congress, and it is this concurrence rather than sanctions or leadership
control, that explains party voting among members of the House and
Senate. (146)

Party elites are not necessarily steered by the party leadership but are
personally ideologically distinctive. In other words, leaders tend "if liberal,
to be more liberal, if conservative, to be more conservative" (Kirkpatrick
1976, 297). Party elites are perhaps more ideologically intense than the
general public because of higher levels of political information and involvement (Eldersveld 1964, 153). Members of Congress as party elites are thus
generally more ideologically extreme than the average voter.

The Republican and Democratic Parties have relatively stable policy
platforms (Ippolito and Walker 1980). "In some policy areas, such as social
welfare, government regulation, economic management, and agricultural
assistance, there have been significant and fairly stable interparty differences
over the years" (ibid., 146). For this reason, it is possible to track the extent
to which Members of Congress articulate the preferences of their party
when voting on domestic issues, by examining Member behavior relative to
these significant, stable different policy issues.

Several groups have created indices by which to measure legislators'
ideological leanings as expressed through their roll-call voting behavior.
Among the most popular are *National Journal*'s vote ratings of Members
across economic, social, and foreign issue dimensions; indexes created by
interest groups such as *Americans for Democratic Action* and *The American
Conservative Union*; and most recently, Poole and Rosenthal's DW-
NOMINATE scores.

A popular measure of party support is provided through the legislative
voting record of Members. *Congressional Quarterly* records a number of "key
votes" each congressional session to compare the voting records of Members
with their espoused political party. "Key votes" are defined as issues that represent "a matter of major controversy, a test of presidential or political power,
[and/or] a decision of potentially great impact on the nation and the lives of
Americans" (Congressional Quarterly Almanac, v33, 1B).

Several studies have assessed the relationship between party membership
and roll-call voting using this *CQ* measure. The extent to which Members
vote in line with their party leadership is considered their party unity score.
Certain factors are thought to influence party unity. Cantor and Herrnson
(1997) suggest that party unity is enhanced by national party assistance in
congressional campaigns. In 1984 and 1992, the Democratic Congressional
Campaign Committee's (DCCC) assistance with campaign communication
of key issues fostered increased party unity in the ensuing congressional

sessions. Similarly, in 1994, "The dramatic increase in Republican party unity during the early days of the 104th Congress was undoubtedly tied to the GOP's unified campaign message" (Cantor and Herrnson 1997, 411; see also Gimpel 1996). Majority status may also lead Members to feel collective responsibility for legislative action and parties to emphasize a unified platform in campaign message creation (Cantor and Herrnson 1997).

Women as Ideological

Focus on the influence of women in legislatures grew out of the feminist movement of the 1970s and women's ascension to political office. Gender theory developed around the ideological and participatory differences between men and women in the legislative arena. Research found that female Members are more interested in promoting women's issue legislation than their male counterparts. It has been suggested that issues concerning the family, child welfare, women's health and reproductive rights, and sex discrimination are all of more interest to women legislators (Carroll 1985; Saint-Germain 1989; Thomas and Welch 1991; Thomas 1994; Dodson 1998; Swers 2002). Consequently, female legislators were thought to have more liberal ideological orientations and vote scores than male legislators (Leader 1977; Welch 1985).

Critics of gender theory point to vacillations in female Members' voting behavior over time. Although women did demonstrate more liberal voting behavior than men during the 1970s, women demonstrated similar voting scores to men during the 1980's (Vega and Firestone 1995). In the early 1990s, and with the Year of the Woman in 1992, however, women once again began to demonstrate more liberal voting records than men (ibid.).

It is possible that this recent pattern is due to constituency factors, partisanship, and ethnicity rather than ideological differences due to gender (Welch 1985; Vega and Firestone 1995). In fact, partisanship explains 91 percent of the variance between men's and women's vote scores (Schwindt 2000). Proportionately, female Members are more Democratic (i.e., liberal) than male Members. Gender, on the other hand, explains only 5 percent of the variance in Members' voting behavior (ibid.).

While the role of gender cannot be dismissed, Schwindt (2000) suggests that:

> it is important to keep in mind that the U.S. political system is based on representation by political parties, not gender, and those political parties will continue to play the most important role in determining the way a representative votes. (11)

In the literature on women and politics, partisanship is often largely neglected as a major influence conditioning a female legislator's vote. While women are more likely to show bipartisan support on issues directly concerning women, such as abortion and women's health (Dolan 1997; Swers 1998), it is important to note that women are not a homogenous group and demonstrate very diverse ideological voting behavior (Swers 2002).

It is also important to recognize that women's issues encompass a broad gamut of issue areas. Anything affecting a woman can be (and often is) classified as a woman's issue. Thus there is need for conceptual clarity in issue identification in gender studies of legislative behavior. Critics suggest that present gender theory fails to distinguish among gender, feminism, and women's interests (Duerst-Lahti 2002). Swers (2000) suggests that we distinguish between "traditional women's issues" such as childcare and women's health, and "feminist issues," which specifically concern women's rights. Consequently, she suggests that women's issues may be categorized as social welfare, feminist, or antifeminist (2002). Because feminist issues are often highly controversial it may be important to consider women's support of these issues separately (Norton 1997; Swers 2000, 2002).

It is possible that feminist issues, especially since the 104th Congress, do not garner the bipartisan support of all congresswomen. For example, the number of amendments concerning reproductive policy increased after 1995 (Norton 2000, 2002). This increase, however, was due to "a smaller group of highly motivated (Democratic) women activists on key subcommittees (who) offered a majority of all reproductive-policy amendments" (2002, 330).

Although the number of women in committees has increased and consequently the support garnered for women's issue policy has increased over the years, the majority of women actively concerned with these issues subsequent to 1994 have held minority status. This observation is crucial to understanding Norton's finding that leadership may have counteracted the positive force of increased female membership in conference committees concerning reproductive rights.

The presence of highly motivated pro-life policy activists like Hyde and Smith, who both held committee and subcommittee leadership positions, may have worked as a counterforce to the increased number of women conferees (ibid., 334).

Ideological Difference

Although gender theory has consistently suggested that women's inclusion in legislative bodies is important because women support feminist issues, undertones yielding these findings suspect are evident in more recent work on gender and legislative behavior. Numerous conservative women elected to the U.S. House of Representatives in 1994 and thereafter have not supported feminist issues, and have actually voted in favor of antifeminist legislation (Swers 2002). Deborah Pryce, a moderate Republican Member elected 1992 just before the Republican Revolution commented on these new extremely conservative female Members, stating:

> I think that some women members feel that they . . . must play up the women's issues for the women's groups back home, for a constituency that really helped them get elected. And so perhaps they get known for those issues more than other things. But in this Congress, especially with this new pack of women, they only shy away from that type of thing, and they want to be known as representatives and not women representatives, and [they believe] that all issues are their issues. (cited in Carroll 2002, 64)

In a discussion of ideological frameworks, Duerst-Lahti (2002) contends that gender constitutes a separate ideological spectrum from the traditional liberal/conservative framework. It is characterized as a "protoideology"— "a parent or source ideology from which other political or governing ideologies emanate" (30). Under the umbrella of gender ideology, therefore, lie both socialism and social conservatism. Both hold a distinctly gendered understanding of the state, one feminal the other masculine. The term "feminal" permits us to capture the broad ideological spectrum of women's interests, referring to that which is female without referring to the loaded term "feminism" (for a detailed discussion, refer to pp. 30–33). It is important to clarify that:

> Gender ideology is more than feminism and feminism is more than one unified political ideology. . . . To recognize this fact is to break free of the notion that feminism is the only gendered political ideology, a recognition that opens the door to more complete analysis. . . . Both men and women hold views that run the ideological spectrum, about governing *and* about gender. (30–31)

"*Feminalism* is defined as an ideology that begins from, and generally prefers, that which is associated with feminality, the feminale and females" (ibid., 31). Duerst-Lahti's anlaysis suggests that the current political context demands reevaluation of our terms, our assumptions, and our theoretical frameworks when examining ideological orientations of female Members of Congress.

Gender theory has only recently begun to address the ideological orientations of female party elites such as Members of Congress. Female party

elites appear to come from similar political orientations as male party elites
("social background, political status, political careers, and perceptions of the
political process") and demonstrate diverse issue orientations (Jennings and
Farah 1981, 462). "Issue orientations . . . continue to be a matter of party
rather than gender" (ibid., 472). Even in the 1960s and 1970s, at the height
of the feminist movement, party and general ideology were better predictors
of preferences with respect to feminist issues than gender. Female
Democratic party elites more often identified with a feminist position than
female Republican party elites, and similarly, male Democratic party elites
more often identified with a feminist position than male Republican party
elites (ibid., 478).

Different Attitudes . . . Similar Perspectives

There are significant partisan differences in the testimony content of female
Members of Congress. In an examination of the welfare debate of the mid-
1990s, female Republican Members were less than half as likely as female
Democratic Members to frame the debate in terms of children (Walsh
2002, 380–381). Similarly, women were significantly more likely to frame
the debate over "partial-birth abortion" in terms of motherhood and
parenting, whereas men framed the debate in terms of the welfare of the
unborn child (ibid., 386). Interestingly, however, women used the frame
of children in the case of welfare reform and motherhood in the case of
"partial-birth abortion" to both support and oppose the legislation based
on personal partisanship (ibid.).

While female Members of Congress have similar perspectives, male and
female Members clearly approach social policy from different perspectives.
Particularly in the case of welfare reform and "partial birth abortion,"
significant differences were revealed between the personal experience
testimonies of men and women. In the case of welfare reform, men
emphasized tax relief and women emphasized the effect of the legislation on
children.

It is reasonable for us to conclude that: (1) women do use similar
perspectives or frames to discuss policy, but (2) women do not necessarily
agree on the policy outcomes they prefer. The importance, therefore, of
understanding issue framing in terms of representation resides not in the
similarity of issue preference but in the similarity of personal experience.
Walsh concludes:

> Women more often than men mention the effect of legislation on underrep-
> resented constituencies, and they bring to the floor firsthand experience of

the difficulties mothers face. Since women act as empathetic delegates of underrepresented concerns, they are transforming Congress into an institution that considers more closely the thoughts and fears of the whole population. Thus, women's perspectives incorporated into debate enlarge the representative nature of the legislative process. (ibid., 390)

When examining gender differences in women's issue bill sponsorship, however, "the influence of gender on a member's legislative behavior is highly dependent on his/her overall political ideology" (Swers 2000, 20). While moderate Republican women are much more likely to sponsor women's issue legislation than their male colleagues, conservative Republican women are not. In 1994, a number of conservative Republican women were elected to Congress. Conservative women can be expected to either ignore women's issues altogether or actively support antifeminist legislation. Although these women appear to be concerned with electoral security rather than women's issues, this behavior could be a result of conscious political choice on the part of conservative Republican congresswomen (ibid.). Citing Miller (1995), Swers suggests:

Given their small numbers in Congress, the conservative women knew that their gender and position on women's issues would gain media attention. Therefore, these women made a point of stating that they did not "claim sisterhood with the so-called 'women's agenda' " and that they viewed themselves as 'citizens' rather than as women. (2002, 274)

It is possible that in the not-so-distant future, when these women gain leadership positions within the Republican Party, conservative women might actually inhibit women's issue legislation (ibid.).

Differences in Voting Behavior

Much of the research on women and Congress focuses on women's activity on feminist and traditional women's issues—those issues directly targeting the status of women and children. Women support these issues through both their formal and informal legislative activities. In terms of a general philosophical ethos, women espouse a more liberal ideological orientation toward the role of government with regard to social welfare and equal rights. Consequently, female representatives as a collective whole illustrate more liberal voting patterns than their male colleagues. Simply looking at women's legislative voting behavior in one year across multiple measures demonstrates this finding.

The measures included for the sake of comparison all represent ideological continuums running from liberal to conservative. Two monitoring entities, Americans for Democratic Action (ADA) and *National Journal* measure voting patterns on a 1–100 scale with 1 representing the most conservative voting behavior and 100 representing the most liberal voting behavior. Contrastingly, the American Conservative Union's scores are on a 1–100 scale with 1 representing the most liberal voting behavior and 100 representing the most conservative voting behavior. Finally, DW-NOMINATE scores are on a scale between −1 and +1 with −1 representing the most liberal and +1 representing the most conservative voting behavior.

Looking at the mean ideological differences between male and female Members across these multiple measures in 2001 illustrates that women vote more liberally than men (see table 3.1). Using Poole and Rosenthal's (1997) measure of ideology, bounded between −1 and +1 with conservatism increasing in a positive direction, we see that women's average vote score (−0.0597) is more liberal than men's average vote score (0.0427). Similarly, the average female legislator's ADA score (53.43) is more liberal than the average male legislator's ADA score (45.76). Even across issue dimensions, we see that women have more liberal voting tendencies on the whole, than men. In terms of economic policy, social policy, and foreign policy, women illustrate more liberal vote patterns than men. The difference, however, is most pronounced in vote averages on social issues. The average female legislator's social liberalism score (55.68) is much more liberal than the average male legislator's social liberalism score (46.24). It is not surprising, therefore, that gender theorists have highlighted this important difference between the ideological leanings of men and women legislators.

The distribution of Members' vote scores by gender, however, does not fit a normal curve, but rather, it mirrors a bimodal distribution. Male legislators either received DW-NOMINATE scores of −.02 or below or .13 or above approximately in the 107th Congress. This is the logical product of ideologically differentiated political parties. The pattern is also the same for female legislators.

Although more female Members are on the liberal end of the spectrum than on the conservative end, the cases are still quite skewed to fit a bimodal distribution. Female legislators either received DW-NOMINATE scores of −.24 or below or .04 or above in the 107th Congress. It should be noted that just as men cross the gamut of ideological difference, so do women. There are female legislators who received DW-NOMINATE scores of −.84 in the 107th Congress; there are female legislators who received DW-NOMINATE scores of .58 in the 107th Congress. The important point to be made is that male and female legislators both illustrate partisan patterns

Table 3.1 Mean ideological differences between male and female members across multiple measures in 2001

		DW-NOMINATE	ADA	Economic liberalism	Social liberalism	Foreign liberalism
Male	Mean	.0831	42.1582	46.8735	44.0062	46.2123
	N	375	373	324	325	325
	s.d.	.4634	40.2775	29.5382	30.6928	29.1511
Female	Mean	−.2245	69.2500	64.6863	67.0769	63.9808
	N	60	60	51	52	52
	s.d.	.4014	37.9431	27.8729	27.1487	30.1860
Total	Mean	.0407	45.9122	49.2960	47.1883	48.6631
	N	435	433	375	377	377
	s.d.	.4671	41.0049	29.9128	31.2281	29.8914

The data for this analysis was taken from a number of sources. I employ the vote scaling techniques developed by Poole and Rosenthal (1985, 1991, 1997). These DW-NOMINATE scores were downloaded from Keith Poole's data archive on the web at: http://voteview.uh.edu/default_nomdata.htm and are recorded for the 103rd through 107th Congresses. DW-NOMINATE scores are useful in that they can be compared across congresses. DW-NOMINATE scores provide a single measure of ideology, bounded between +1 and −1 with conservatism increasing in a positive direction on a single left-right continuum. ADA scores were taken from the website of the Americans for Democratic Action at http://adaction.org/voting.html. The three liberalism measures were compiled from the website of National Journal at http://nationaljournal.com/ and required membership to access. Refer to the section in the introduction for a more thorough presentation of data sources.

of ideological voting behavior. Party is a more obvious determinant of ideology than gender.

The literature suggests that female Members are more liberal on social issues than male Members. Male Members received social ratings across the board in the 107th Congress just as they did DW-NOMINATE scores. Although the ratings ranged from 0 to 90 percent, the average male social rating was 44.01 percent with a standard deviation of 30.69. Standard deviation measures the extent to which the cases under analysis vary from the mean. Within one standard deviation of the mean are usually about 68 percent of cases, and within two standard deviations are about 95 percent of cases. So we can see that 68 percent of male Members of Congress fall between 17.19 and 74.01 on a 100-point scale. In other words, there is a wide range in the scores of male Members of Congress. They are not a very homogenous group.

The distribution of male ratings is fairly even across the spectrum. Contrastingly, female Members' ratings were by and large on the liberal end of the spectrum. Although the ratings also ranged from 0 to 90 percent, the mean female rating was 67.08 percent with a standard deviation of 27.15. This mean is 23 percentage points higher than the mean score for male Members, indicating that in general women are more liberal than men on social issues.

Partisanship and Women's Ideological Voting Behavior

While on the whole women are more liberal than men in terms of their voting behavior, simple distributions reveal that both men and women demonstrate bimodal or partisan patterns of ideological voting. In order to examine the partisan contours of women's voting behavior more thoroughly, I examined Democratic ideological voting and Republican ideological voting separately. The theoretical importance of this section is to examine how women participate in the legislative arena (one measure being "voting behavior") as compared to their male partisan colleagues.

In chapter 2, we discovered that while Members operate in a partisan climate, they also operate in a climate conditioned by their electoral security. We also discovered that electoral security for women varies substantially by party. Republican women perceive themselves as representing competitive districts, and this vulnerability shapes their legislative activity. Democratic women, on the other hand, do not perceive themselves in very competitive districts, by and large, and thus enjoy more personal discretion in their legislative pursuits. Consequently, in this chapter, we examine the ideological voting behavior of Democratic and Republican women separately, and also examine the impact of electoral vulnerability on women's ideological behavior.

Before separating the pooled data for this analysis, Chow tests were run on the regression equations to determine whether or not there are significant differences in the coefficients attributable to the parties. This statistical procedure uses the F-statistic to compare differences in the pooled regression and separated regressions. The results indicate that the coefficients for Democrats and Republicans are not equal, and thus the data should not be pooled. While theoretically we might assume that the same variables predict ideological voting behavior, the relative impact of those variables is not the same for Democrats and Republicans.

Democratic Ideological Voting

The distributions of Democratic male and female DW-NOMINATE scores illustrate the findings of chapter 2. Democratic men are rather ideologically diverse—their scores ranging from $-.88$ to $+.20$. The average DW-NOMINATE score among Democratic men is $-.39$, and the standard deviation is .18. By contrast, Democratic women are rather ideologically homogenous as a group. Democratic women score from $-.84$ to $-.24$. At $-.47$, the mean score among Democratic women is also more liberal than that of Democratic men, and the standard deviation is only .12.

The distribution of Democratic Members' social liberalism scores illustrates the more liberal voting tendencies of Democratic women suggested by the literature. Democratic men have social liberalism ratings ranging from 0 to 90 percent. With the majority of men receiving ratings above 50 percent, the mean rating of this group is 71.23 percent, with a standard deviation of 15.80. Contrastingly, Democratic women have scores ranging from 68 to 90 percent. With a mean of 82.56 percent, the standard deviation of this group is only 6.74, suggesting that Democratic women are much more liberal and much more homogenous as a group than Democratic men.

Developing a Model of Voting Behavior

Several factors are understood to be associated with Member voting behavior and should be incorporated into any predictive model. The three variables of theoretical interest to the analysis at hand are: Member partisanship, gender, and electoral security. Beyond these, we know that seniority is significantly associated with voting behavior (Brewer, Mariani, and Stonecash 2002). Also, several district characteristics are important influences on voting behavior. In this analysis, the size of the district's African American population as well as socioeconomic indicators, such as the average per capita income, percent college educated, and percent rural population of the district, were examined.

These socioeconomic indicators, however, are known to be correlated. Consequently, factor analysis was conducted for purposes of data reduction. Given the significant associations found in the correlation matrix, a series of variables were examined using factor analysis to test the stability of the component created from the three variables of interest. Employing an Eigenvalue cut-point of 1.0, a single component was drawn from the three variables. This single component was included as a variable in the regression models to measure the socioeconomic character of the district. The principal component analysis explains about 72.204 percent of the total variance in these three variables.

Finally, the presidential vote is included to capture the influence of the general ideological orientation of the district on Member behavior (Bianco

1984; Bond, Covington, and Fleischer 1985; Canon 1990). While this measure is the subject of debate, it is the most consistent data source available that measures voter preferences at the district level. Because it is based on voting behavior, it provides a more accurate indicator of the political character of the district than those provided by demographic characteristics (Bond, Campbell, and Cottrill 2001, 12). While some have used the mean presidential vote across multiple elections in order to limit the idiosyncratic effects of individual candidates (Bianco 1984), critics of this measure argue that doing so reduces the accuracy of the measure in capturing contemporary leanings (Bond, Campbell, and Cottrill 2001, 11).

The present analysis examines both demographic and political indicators of district preferences. Why should we expect district variables to predict Member behavior? As Fiorina suggests, "Those representatives who grossly misjudge the empirical situation do not survive long in the electoral arena" (1974, 40).

The first model predicts the DW-NOMINATE scores or ideological voting behavior of Democratic Members given the electoral security of the Member as well as other Member- and district-level factors (see table 3.2). The model explains nearly half of the variance in Member voting behavior across congresses (adj. R^2 ranging from .425 in the 105th Congress to .506 in the 103rd Congress). While the seniority of the Member is a significant predictor of voting behavior in the 105th and 106th Congresses (significant at the .01 level), in general the Member-level indicators are rather insignificant. Member electoral vulnerability or marginality, for example, is not significant after the 103rd Congress, and is only significant then at the $p < .05$ level.

Contrastingly, the district-level variables are generally significant predictors of Member voting behavior. While the size of the black population in the district is not a significant predictor after the 103rd Congress, the socioeconomic character as well as the district presidential vote return are both consistently significant predictors of Member voting behavior (significant for the most part at least at the $p < .01$ level). The most important observation to be made is that gender is not a significant predictor of voting behavior in any congress. While the slope is in the predicted direction—a more liberal direction—when controlling for other factors, gender is not significantly associated with ideological voting.

The pattern is basically the same when examining Member voting behavior on social issues. While the Member-level variables are generally insignificant, the district indicators are generally significantly related to Democratic Member voting behavior. While the size of the black population in the district is not significant, once again both the socioeconomic character and the presidential vote return are significantly associated with

Table 3.2 Predicting DW-NOMINATE scores of democratic members given electoral marginality

	103rd Congress *b* (s.e.)	104th Congress *b* (s.e.)	105th Congress *b* (s.e.)	106th Congress *b* (s.e.)	107th Congress *b* (s.e.)
Constant	.220 (.049)	.153 (.058)	.100 (.059)	.154 (.058)	−.853 (.069)
Sex	−.027 (.026)	−.022 (.028)	−.045 (.026)	−.040 (.024)	−.023 (.034)
Seniority	−.002 (.001)	−.002 (.001)	−.003 (.001)**	−.003 (.001)**	−.002 (.001)
Marginality	−.045 (.019)*	−.022 (.021)	.009 (.021)	−.035 (.022)	.001 (.029)
% Black	.135 (.064)*	.089 (.067)	−.006 (.064)	.027 (.060)	.176 (.073)*
Socioeconomic factor	−.025 (.009)**	−.030 (.010)**	−.026 (.010)**	−.023 (.010)*	.003 (.014)
Presidential vote return	−1.125 (.101)***	−.995 (.113)***	−.763 (.103)***	−.858 (.101)***	1.112 (.150)***
Adj. R^2	.506 (.1280)	.484 (.1260)	.425 (.1310)	.440 (.1237)	.386 (.1354)
Valid N	245	193	196	203	160
Durbin-Watson	1.803	1.810	2.013	1.967	2.041

* $p < .05$ level
** $p < .01$ level
*** $p < .001$ level

Throughout the analysis, the standard error is reported in parentheses.

social ratings (significant across congresses at the $p < .001$ level except for once when still significant at the $p < .01$ level). One difference between the models, however, is that while gender is not a significant predictor of DW-NOMINATE scores, it is sometimes a significant predictor of social ratings. In the 105th and 106th Congresses, Democratic females received significantly higher social liberalism ratings than Democratic men (significant at least at the $p < .05$ level). When we examine the interaction effects between gender and electoral security in predicting DW-NOMINATE scores and social ratings among Democratic Members, we find that electoral vulnerability is not a significant influence on female Members' behavior (see table 3.3). In other words, Democratic women are significantly more likely to vote more liberally on social issues at times than their male colleagues, even given circumstantial differences such as their own personal electoral vulnerability.

Republican Ideological Voting

Among Republicans, the pattern is very similar between men and women except it is in a more conservative distribution overall. Republican men have DW-NOMINATE scores ranging from .13 to 1.29, with the average Member having a vote score of .48. The standard deviation among Republican men is .16. Republican women have similar scores ranging from .04 to .58. At .35, the average score among Republican women is .13 points more liberal than that among Republican men. The standard deviation in this group is smaller than the standard deviation among Republican men (.14). This pattern is the same as that between Democratic men and women. Democratic women are more ideologically homogenous as a group than Democratic men, and here we find that Republican women are more homogenous as a group than Republican men.

In examining Republican Members' social liberalism ratings, the differences between male and female Members are in the expected direction. With liberal scores ranging between 0 and 63 percent, Republican men are socially conservative. Even within the range of ratings, the distribution is toward the conservative end of the scale. The average Republican male Member received a social liberalism rating of 21.24 percent in the 107th Congress. The standard deviation in this group was 19.53.

Republican women, on the other hand, demonstrate a much different pattern. With ratings ranging from 0 to 60 percent, Republican women demonstrate more liberal social ratings than Republican men. The distribution is skewed more toward the liberal end of the scale, than that of Republican men. The mean rating among Republican women is

Table 3.3 Predicting DW-NOMINATE scores of democratic members given female electoral marginality

	103rd Congress b (s.e.)	104th Congress b (s.e.)	105th Congress b (s.e.)	106th Congress b (s.e.)	107th Congress b (s.e.)
Constant	.214 (.049)	.153 (.058)	.100 (.059)	23.823 (6.169)	−.854 (.069)
Sex	−.054 (.035)	−.029 (.034)	−.041 (.031)	4.786 (2.933)	−.033 (.042)
Seniority	−.001 (.001)	−.002 (.001)	−.003 (.001)**	−.053 (.121)	−.002 (.001)
Marginality	−.051 (.020)**	−.024 (.022)	.011 (.022)	.502 (2.520)	−.004 (.031)
Marginal females	.058 (.050)	.021 (.055)	−.012 (.052)	4.347 (5.256)	.029 (.067)
% Black	.130 (.064)*	.087 (.067)	−.006 (.065)	−5.895 (6.221)	.178 (.073)*
Socioeconomic factor	−.027 (.009)**	−.030 (.010)**	−.025 (.010)*	5.178 (.987)***	.003 (.014)
Presidential vote return	−1.109 (.102)***	−.993 (.114)***	−.764 (.103)***	80.569 (10.669)***	1.117 (.151)***
Adj. R^2	.507 (.1279)	.482 (.1263)	.422 (.1313)	.479 (12.5558)	.383 (.1358)
Valid N	245	193	196	188	160
Durbin-Watson	1.825	1.811	2.011	1.973	2.048

* $p < .05$ level
** $p < .01$ level
*** $p < .001$ level

32.25 percent—11 points higher than that of Republican men. At 23.05, the standard deviation is slightly larger than the standard deviation for Republican men, but interestingly it is much larger than that among Democratic women (6.74). Although more liberal overall than Republican men, this pattern indicates that Republican women are much more heterogeneous or diverse in voting behavior on social issues than Democratic women.

In estimating the model to predict Republican Members' DW-NOMINATE scores, several differences between the two models are evident (see table 3.4). First, the model explains much less of Republican voting behavior than Democratic voting behavior. The model explains roughly a quarter of the variance in Republican Member behavior, with the adj. R^2 ranging from .238 in the 107th Congress to .281 in the 103rd Congress. Another important difference concerns the significance of Member-level indicators. While Member-level variables were not generally significant predictors of Democratic scores, they are significant predictors of Republican scores. Women are at times significantly more liberal than their male copartisans. More senior Members are significantly more liberal than more junior Members (significant at least at the $p < .05$ level across all congresses). In nearly all congresses, electoral security is also significantly associated with voting behavior. Though we might expect marginal Members to demonstrate more liberal voting behavior, following the moderate tendencies of their constituencies, this is not the case. Marginal Members are significantly more conservative than safe Members (significant in most congresses at least at the $p < .05$ level). Further in contrast to the Democratic model, district-level characteristics are not generally significantly related to Republican ideological voting. Only the presidential vote return of the district is consistently significant in predicting vote scores (significant at the $p < .001$ level).

Predicting Republican social ratings produces somewhat different findings. While female Members' social ratings reflect female Members' DW-NOMINATE scores, seniority is not significant in predicting social ratings. Electoral security is sometimes significant, with more marginal Members voting more conservatively on social issues at times. The association between district-level characteristics and Republican Member voting behavior also differs from that in the model predicting DW-NOMINATE scores. The socioeconomic character of the district as well as its presidential vote return are both fairly consistently and significantly associated with social ratings. Also, the black population in the district is significant at the $p < .01$ level beginning in the 106th Congress. Overall, the model is weaker than previous models, only explaining between .169 and .368 of the variance in voting behavior on social issues across congresses.

The next question to answer is how Republican women, finding themselves in more competitive districts, facing greater electoral uncertainty than

Table 3.4 Predicting DW-NOMINATE scores of Republicans given electoral marginality

	103rd Congress b (s.e.)	104th Congress b (s.e.)	105th Congress b (s.e.)	106th Congress b (s.e.)	107th Congress b (s.e.)
Constant	.833 (.063)	.966 (.064)	1.005 (.069)	1.009 (.068)	−.070 (.084)
Sex	−.135 (.038)***	−.059 (.035)	−.066 (.037)	−.071 (.036)*	−.098 (.036)**
Seniority	−.004 (.001)**	−.005 (.001)***	−.006 (.001)***	−.004 (.001)**	−.003 (.002)*
Marginality	.064 (.021)**	.062 (.023)**	.021 (.021)	.076 (.023)***	.046 (.024)*
% Black	−.277 (.198)	.151 (.169)	−.071 (.149)	.121 (.158)	.080 (.118)
Socioeconomic factor	−.007 (.010)	−.024 (.010)**	−.006 (.010)	−.008 (.010)	.011 (.010)
Presidential vote return	−01.081 (.171)***	−1.333 (.175)***	−1.141 (.159)***	−1.203 (.161)***	.980 (.137)***
Adj. R^2	.281 (.1253)	.260 (.1355)	.246 (.1427)	.266 (.1371)	.238 (.1427)
Valid N	165	217	213	207	216
Durbin–Watson	1.682	1.643	2.026	1.952	1.975

* $p < .05$ level
** $p < .01$ level
*** $p < .001$ level

their male copartisan colleagues, vote? In examining the interaction effects between gender and electoral security, we find that electorally vulnerable female Republican Members illustrate significantly different ideological voting patterns than marginal male Republicans or safe female Republicans (see table 3.5). Both gender and electoral security, however, are independently significant. This finding suggests that when controlling for the significant influence of seniority, more safe females were significantly more liberal than their other Republican colleagues from the 103rd to the 105th Congresses (significant at the $p < .05$ level). It appears, however, that this trend is somewhat related to turnover; in the 106th and 107th Congresses Republican women representing safe districts vote no differently than men in safe districts.

Contrastingly, Republican men representing vulnerable seats are significantly more conservative than their fellow Republican colleagues (significant across most congresses at least at the $p < .05$ level). Republican women representing vulnerable districts are not significantly more liberal or conservative than we might expect given both their gender and their electoral security. In other words, these women act both like Republican women, and like Republican Members representing vulnerable congressional seats.

Predicting social ratings among Republican Members, there a few significant differences. First, gender is significantly related to voting behavior in different congresses compared with the model predicting DW-NOMINATE scores. In the previous model (see table 3.5), the gender of the Members was significant in the 103rd through the 105th Congresses. In predicting social liberalism, the gender of the Member is significant in the 103rd and the 105th through 107th Congresses, but not in the 104th Congress. Finally, while in predicting DW-NOMINATE scores, there are no significant interaction effects between gender and marginality, in predicting social ratings in the 105th Congress electorally marginal females are significantly more conservative than we would expect given their gender and electoral security independently (significant at the $p < .05$ level).

It should also be noted that the district measures also perform differently in predicting the two measures. While the size of the African American population in the district is never significantly associated with DW-NOMINATE scores, it is very significant in predicting social ratings in the 106th and 107th Congresses (significant at the $p < .01$ level). Interestingly, however, the slope is not in the direction we might expect. As the African American population in the district increases, the social rating of the Member decreases. In other words, a larger minority population is associated with a more conservative social rating. There are also discrepancies between the models regarding the influence of district socioeconomic

Table 3.5 Predicting DW-NOMINATE scores of Republicans given female electoral marginality

	103rd Congress b (s.e.)	104th Congress b (s.e.)	105th Congress b (s.e.)	106th Congress b (s.e.)	107th Congress b (s.e.)
Constant	.833 (.063)	.960 (.065)	1.007 (.069)	1.009 (.068)	−.071 (.085)
Sex	−.136 (.060)*	−.090 (.045)*	−.105 (.053)*	−.079 (.043)	−.078 (.046)
Seniority	−.004 (.001)**	−.005 (.001)***	−.006 (.001)***	−.004 (.001)**	−.003 (.002)*
Marginality	.064 (.022)**	.055 (.024)*	.015 (.022)	.074 (.024)**	.051 (.025)*
Marginal females	.002 (.078)	.075 (.070)	.075 (.073)	.027 (.077)	−.052 (.073)
% Black	−.277 (.199)	.155 (.169)	−.064 (.149)	.122 (.159)	.084 (.118)
Socioeconomic factor	−.007 (.010)	−.023 (.010)*	−.005 (.010)	−.007 (.010)	.011 (.010)
Presidential vote return	−1.080 (.173)***	−1.310 (.176)***	−1.141 (.159)***	−1.199 (.161)***	.979 (.137)***
Adj. R^2	.276 (.1257)	.260 (.1355)	.246 (.1427)	.263 (.1374)	.236 (.1428)
Valid N	165	217	213	207	216
Durbin-Watson	1.682	1.355	2.027	1.947	1.958

* $p < .05$ level
** $p < .01$ level
*** $p < .001$ level

characteristics on Member voting behavior. While the socioeconomic character of the district is only slightly significant in predicting DW-NOMINATE
scores in the 104th Congress, this variable is highly significant in predicting
social ratings in both the 104th and 106th Congresses (significant at the
$p < .001$ level). In sum, it appears that Republicans are much more likely
to reflect constituent interests when voting on social issues.

Do Women Vote with the Party?

This pattern is mirrored when looking at formal measures of party support.
On average, party unity scores for the full House have been between 84.95
and 89.93 (see table 3.6). Interestingly, the parties were most unified in
1999 and 2001, the last two years of the sample. Party unity scores in these
two years on average surpassed party unity scores even in 1995—the 104th
Congress touted as the most partisan congress in decades. It is not com-
pletely accurate to conclude that the present atmosphere is more partisan
than that of the Republican Revolution. A more accurate understanding
would compare the strict party unity of Republicans and the limited unity
of Democrats in 1995 with the relatively equal and high levels of unity
characteristic of the current period.

In the 103rd Congress, prior to the Republican takeover of the House in
1994, Democrats were on average more unified than Republicans. After
1994, however, the pattern reversed with Republicans consistently having
higher average party unity scores than Democrats from 1995 to 2001. Party
unity declined among Democrats between 1993 and 1996, but between
1997 and 2001 it steadily increased and reached an all-time high (for the
sample years) in 2001 of 85.91. Republican party unity surged in 1995 to a
remarkable 91.10, paralleled pre-majority scores in 1998 at 84.82 (1993
was 84.80), but increased again into the 1990s in 2001 (93.73) surpassing
the infamous unity of 1995.

Female party unity scores were on average higher than male party unity
scores in all years in the sample. This difference was greatest in 1993 with
men voted with the party 84.78 percent of the time and women 87.32 percent of the time. Republican men have been on average five points higher
than Republican women since gaining the majority. In 1993 and 1994,
however, this difference was nearly double, averaging ten percentage points.
Democratic women have been on average at least seven points higher than
Democratic men.

Party unity was at an all-time low in 1995 for Democratic males (79.43)
and in 1997 for Democratic females (87.62), and was at an all-time high in

Table 3.6 Mean party unity based on partisanship and sex of member: 1993–2001

		1993	1995	1997	1999	2001
Republican	Mean	84.80	91.10	87.82	88.10	93.73
	N	176	230	227	222	225
	s.d.	9.95	5.96	9.05	8.25	5.71
Democrat	Mean	85.23	80.69	81.78	85.49	85.91
	N	256	203	205	212	214
	s.d.	10.45	14.99	12.39	13.38	12.92
Male	Mean	84.78	86.07	84.76	86.55	89.63
	N	385	386	378	378	380
	s.d.	10.19	12.55	11.42	11.31	11.14
Female	Mean	87.32	87.43	86.31	88.64	91.77
	N	47	47	54	56	60
	s.d.	10.45	9.86	9.17	9.71	6.31
Republican male	Mean	85.49	91.46	88.12	88.58	94.09
	N	164	213	211	205	207
	s.d.	9.45	5.45	8.79	7.75	5.15
Republican female	Mean	75.33	86.53	83.88	82.35	89.61
	N	12	17	16	17	18
	s.d.	12.16	9.49	11.58	11.76	9.34
Democratic male	Mean	84.25	79.43	80.49	84.16	84.26
	N	221	173	168	173	172
	s.d.	10.70	15.35	12.85	14.09	13.77
Democratic female	Mean	91.43	87.93	87.62	91.38	92.69
	N	35	30	37	39	42
	s.d.	5.64	10.19	7.82	7.26	4.22
Total	Mean	85.06	86.22	84.95	86.82	89.93
	N	432	433	432	434	440
	s.d.	10.24	12.28	11.17	11.13	10.63

2001 for both groups (men = 84.26; women = 92.69). Party unity was at an all-time low in 1993 for Republican males (85.49) and Republican females (75.33), and was at an all-time high in 2001 for both groups (males = 94.09; females = 89.61). In all years included in the sample, however, Democratic women are more unified with their party than Republican women. Democratic women are between four to sixteen points on average more unified with their party than Republican women. The two notable exceptions are 1995 (Republican women = 86.53; Democratic women = 87.93) and 2001 (Republican women = 89.61; Democratic women = 92.69).

Conclusion

In addressing women's general ideological voting behavior, this analysis indicates that, for the most part, women act like partisans. Democratic women illustrate the same voting patterns as Democratic men, and Republican women illustrate the same voting patterns as Republican men. The exception to this generalization arises in predicting voting behavior on social issues.

Women, both Republican and Democratic, appear to vote more liberally than men on social issues while generally adhering ideologically to the party line. While this finding is nothing new, it is significant in light of the attention given in this chapter to both Member- and district-level characteristics. Particular attention has been paid to the behavior of female legislators given their partisanship. While this preliminary analysis does not advance our understanding of women's actual status and participation within the party organization, it does illuminate the general ideological differences between men and women in terms of voting behavior.

The second general finding of this chapter is that parties matter. Partisanship shapes ideological voting in discernable ways. Party culture determines the amount of discretion Members have in shaping their personal legislative behavior. When applied to legislative behavior, principal-agent theory suggests that Members of Congress are the agents of several principals, including: political parties, constituencies, and interest groups (Parker 1992). In this analysis, the concept of "discretion" is used to describe the amount of freedom Members enjoy from their various principles to pursue their legislative goals. Sometimes the constraints of one principal negatively impact the desires of another principal. In other words, sometimes districts (as principals) restrain Members from responding to party pressures (another principal).

Democratic Party culture provides Members with the discretion or freedom to respond to constituency pressures. We see from this chapter that Democrats do respond to these pressures. Constituency factors as well as personal factors explain half of the variance in Democratic Member's vote decisions. On the other hand, Republican Party culture promotes loyalty and ideological homogeneity and does not provide Members with the discretion to respond to constituency pressures. In other words, Republican Party culture restricts the amount of freedom Members have to pursue goals, whether those be personal or constituent driven. Consequently, Republicans do not respond to district pressures to the same extent as Democrats. In fact, constituency factors as well as personal factors only account for about a quarter of the variance in Republican Members' vote decisions.

Second, this chapter further provides support for party culture theory in that Democrats and Republicans respond to different constituency pressures. In the models, the only common significant predictor between the two parties was the general ideology of the district. Beyond that, the slopes of the indicators predicting Democratic Members' behavior were different in direction and significance from the slopes of the indicators predicting Republican Members' behavior.

These findings yield support for the idea that constituency constraints faced by Members vary by party. These constraints also vary by issue. While the African American population in the district was a significant predictor of general ideological voting behavior among Democrats, it was not a significant predictor of ideological voting on social issues for Democrats. Similarly, while the seniority of Republican Members was significantly associated with their general ideological voting behavior, it was not significantly associated with their voting behavior on social issues. If true, the implications of this finding are theoretically significant for the study of representation. It is useful to once again consider the words of Miller and Stokes:

> Especially critical is the question whether different models of representation apply to different public issues. Is the saliency of legislative action to the public so different in quality and degree on different issues that the legislator have a single generalized mode of response to his constituency that is rooted in a normative belief about the representative's role or does the same legislator respond to his constituency differently on different issues? More evidence is needed on matters so fundamental to our system. (1999, 88)

These implications are also significant for modeling of Member legislative behavior. The scaling technique developed by Poole and Rosenthal has been widely used in the literature because it is highly collinear or correlated with other measures of ideology. It is touted as a general measure that not only encompasses a variety of issue dimensions, but also allows for comparisons across congresses. The present analysis calls into question the generalizability of this measure. Differences between the associations in the models predicting DW-NOMINATE scores and social liberalism ratings suggest that certain questions require multiple measures of ideology. We must recognize the limited utility of this measure, and verify results by comparing measures of ideological voting behavior.

In the end, although gender theory has assumed a cohesive women's voice concerning women's issues, there is reason to believe that women represent diverse constituencies that frame their preferences and behavior in different ways. Republican women are not the same in ideological orientation as Democratic women. However Republican women are most likely to agree with Democrats on social issues, particularly women's issues (Swers 1998, 2002). One Republican woman made these remarks in discussing her Democratic female colleagues:

> I am totally different in philosophy. I am against big government. We agree that we need a degree of a safety net, but people prefer to empower themselves. Republicans are for cutting taxes and regulation. Theirs is such a different philosophy.

It does not follow, however, that women's participation in the legislative arena is inconsequential. Women's inclusion in public debate is important because they bring different experiences, attitudes, and resources to the political table (Tamerius 1995). Some female Members I interviewed expressed the opinion that although women differ in terms of ideology, they are more similar in terms of priorities. One Democratic female Member stated:

> I see them (female Republican Members) as very different (ideologically) because most of them are pro-life. We are ideologically very different, although they (like us) are probably inclusive in the sense that they go to things . . . they probably start out and remain a part of their community. Women members pay more attention to what's going on in the office. Women are more likely to look at a broader range of budget issues . . . they may have different priorities, such as education, housing, and healthcare. Women approach legislating from a different perspective.

Similarly, one Democratic African American female Member remarked:

> In some ways, there is no difference. As a human being, there is no difference. We just differ in what we give priority to. They don't have less ideals about service to constituents. I may be considered far more liberal (for example pro-choice), but some of them are too. We are ideologically different on wealth, income, social programs, and the role of government.

While the simple conclusion to be drawn is that women are more liberal than their male partisan colleagues, the more critical point stems from our examination of party unity scores. Democratic women are much more formally unified with their party than Republican women. On average, women in the Democratic Party support the party position at much higher rates than Democratic men. Conversely, women in the Republican Party support the party position at much lower rates than Republican men. From chapter 2, it is clear that Republican women face electoral pressures very different from those faced by Democratic women. We would expect that Republican women would have lower party support scores than Republican men. The critical question is this: If women do face different pressures and engage in different patterns of voting behavior when taking into consideration partisanship, then what are the implications for their status and participation within the legislative arena? In chapter 4 we examine the positional and participatory differences between men and women within the party organizations of Congress.

Chapter 4

Does Partisanship Shape Women's Participation in the Party Organization?
The Organizational Connection

Rep. Marge Roukema (R-NJ) was passed over by Republican leadership for the chairmanship of the Banking Committee, of which she was the most senior member. She was also one of the most senior female Republicans in the House of Representatives during the 107th Congress and the most senior member on the committee. After she learned the news, she issued the following statement:

> I am gravely disappointed at the decision of the Steering Committee. However, I will be gracious and a good sport as a member of the Republican Team. I pledge to continue my services on the Committee and assure with my knowledge and experience that we protect the safety and soundness of financial services and assure that we continue supplementing the good economy with sound monetary policy. (Roukema Statement on Banking Committee Chairmanship January 4, 2001)

Introduction

In the preceding chapters, we explored the extent to which partisanship shapes the unique pressures women face at the electoral level. These electoral pressures in turn translate into voting behavior within the institution that uniquely positions women within their respective parties.

For Democratic women, electoral pressures fall in line with partisan pressures. In turn, they mirror their male colleagues ideologically and are even more unified in their voting behavior with the party than Democratic men. For Republican women, on the other hand, electoral pressures can conflict with partisan pressures. Consequently, they are sometimes significantly more liberal and significantly less unified with the party in terms of their voting behavior than Republican men.

In this chapter, we examine the organizational connection, including the status and participation of women, within the party organizations. We might expect Democratic women to be equally incorporated within the party organization because of their electoral discretion and ideological consonance with the party. We might expect Republican women conversely to be unequally incorporated within the party organization because of their lack of electoral discretion and ideological dissonance with the party. This chapter is critical to the argument of this book as well as to gender theory because it provides a novel understanding of women's legislative behavior as shaped by partisan participation within the Congress.

In the following pages, we examine the theoretical basis for such an analysis, exploring factors contributing to Member participation and support within party organizations and our present understanding of women's participation within political institutions. From this review, we develop a certain expectation of women's incorporation within the party organizations and so turn to examine the current status of women within the parties. Next, women's participation in party-building activities is presented to measure actual organizational behavior. Finally, we explore the less formal or tangible contours of women's participation within the party organization, such as Member evaluations of the party organizations, perceived roles within the parties, and reflections on gender differences within the context of partisanship.

Party Organizations and Member Support

Too little attention has been given to the advantages held by the majority party in "structuring the committee system—setting up jurisdictions, allocating resources, assigning members, and so forth" (Cox and McCubbins 1993, 8). Just as Members have individual goals that motivate their legislative behavior, so parties have collective goals that motivate leadership behavior. Party leaders use their resources to "promote committee accountability," to "advance or delay legislative initiatives," to "structure the choice context," "to protect prefloor logrolling," and to "reduce uncertainty" (Evans and Oleszek 1999, 120–121). Parties are allowed to pursue these goals because they prove mutually beneficial to Members.

> These simple facts—that majority status can be made preferable to minority status, that leading can be made preferable to following—suggest a rather different view of the motivation of rational legislators . . . Reelection remains important, but its importance can be modified significantly by the desire for *internal advancement*—defined both in terms of a party's advancement to majority status and in terms of the individual MC's advancement in the hierarchy of (committee and leadership) posts within her party. (Cox and McCubbins 1993, 126)

In sum, deference to the party leadership helps Members solve the collective-action problems inherent in the organization (Cox and McCubbins 1993).

Members are motivated to support the party by a number of both external and internal factors, such as committee assignments, legislative support, and campaign funding. Some have even related the strength of party government in the House to a "legislative cartel" (ibid.). In this sense, parties are organizational blocs that cultivate and mobilize support in spite of individual Member and committee interests. "These cartels usurp the power, theoretically resident in the House, to make rules governing the structure and process of legislation" (ibid., 2). Parties have a number of electoral and institutional resources at their disposal to influence Member support. Since the formal and informal reforms implemented by the Republicans in the 104th Congress, the party has taken on a new importance in setting the legislative agenda and influencing legislative behavior. Through a combination of electoral, structural, and political incentives, the contemporary party (particularly the majority party) influences the support of its Members. We see differences in the partisan behavior of Members based on both the institutional status of the Member and the cultural norms of the Member's party organization.

Member Status

A principal tenet of legislative behavior theory is that Members of Congress are driven by a desire to win reelection (Fenno 1973; Mayhew 1974a; Fiorina 1977). Any list of factors contributing to party support through legislative behavior must include, if not begin with, the "electoral connection." Members who represent marginal districts have a greater need for the monetary as well as political support available through the national party organizations. Nonetheless, they suffer from additional electoral pressures that guide their voting behavior. For this reason, marginality of districts has been shown to be associated with lower party support scores (Shannon 1968a; Ansolabehere, Snyder, and Stewart 2001). Even in an era of inter-party competition, such as the modern era, district marginality is associated with lower party support scores (Brady 1973, 155). Members who represent relatively safe districts, on the other hand, do not have this pressing need and can enjoy the additional discretion that electoral security provides (Parker 1992).

There is historical evidence to suggest that party leadership through the Committee on Committees seeks to achieve a number of goals through the committee assignment process such as: management, constituent interest, party maintenance, and party support (Rohde and Shepsle 1973, 905). "It is useful to view the assignment process as an institutionalized allocation process involving goal-seeking actors, scarce but valued commodities, and behavioral constraints" (ibid.). A central goal in the assignment process is to facilitate the reelection of Members (Masters 1961; Clapp 1964). In particular, freshmen from marginal districts benefit from the reelection goal, receiving assignments that benefit their chances of reelection. Even when freshmen do not immediately receive their preferred committee assignment, almost all Members secure preferred positions by their third term (Gertzog 1976).

While there are a number of factors that are considered in committee assignments, such as: the Member's expertise; stances on committee-relevant issues, and seniority; the demographic and factional balance of the committee, and the preferences of the chairman, "being in good graces of the party leader is certainly important in getting on major committees" [(Masters 1961, 345); see (Masters 1961) as well as (Clapp 1964, 207–240) and (Goodwin 1959) for a discussion of factors relevant to committee assignment]. Particularly regarding the major committees, assignment is restricted to more senior Members "who are 'responsible' legislators, and who represent districts which do not require them to take inflexible positions on controversial issues" (Masters 1961, 357). In contrast, "unfavorable assignments, of little political value to the recipients, are sometimes deliberately given by the powers that be as a mark of disapproval, or for reasons that might be described as 'for the good of the order' " (ibid., 356). Interestingly, prior to the realignment of Southern Democratic seats, these conservative members were "less successful in obtaining desired assignments" than their colleagues from other regions (Bullock 1973, 115). They were also required to serve longer than others before being promoted to exclusive committees (ibid.).

The assignment of committee seats illustrates differences in the two party cultures. Since taking over the Congress Republicans have used the committee system as a means for reward and punishment. In the 104th Congress, Republican Speaker Newt Gingrich bypassed several senior Members to appoint loyal partisans to prestigious committee assignments and chairmanships (see Aldrich and Rohde 2000). Contrastingly, Democrats have traditionally based committee assignments strictly on seniority. These differences hold implications not only for party unity but also for the fate of women within the respective organizations.

A group of Members we might expect to illustrate heightened party unity is that of committee chairmen. Since the congressional reforms of the 1970s, committee chairs have illustrated significantly higher levels of party support. In the pre-reform House, it was quite typical for committee chairs to vote with the party less than half of the time. According to Brandes Crook and Hibbing (1985):

> Committee chairmen often registered party support scores of 40, 30 and sometimes even 20 per cent. After William Colmer of Mississippi became chairman of the Rules Committee in 1967 he proceeded to record party support scores of 19 per cent, 25 per cent and 19 per cent in the next three congresses. (225)

In the 1970s the committee system underwent extensive reform intended to strip committee chairmen of their power and strengthen the power held by subcommittees. This move was embodied in the "Subcommittee Bill of Rights" (see Rohde 1974; Hall and Evans 1990). Full committee chairs were no longer able to change the number, composition, and chairs of subcommittees at will, and the jurisdictions of subcommittees were fixed by a full vote of the committee at large. Since the reforms, however, chairs seem more cooperative and willing to follow party leadership (ibid.; Waldman 1980). This behavior is a direct result of changes in the seniority system brought about by congressional reform. Now that there is an incentive structure, committee chairs are much more likely to respond to party pressures. Brandes Crook and Hibbing (1985) suggest:

> The heightened party support of these individuals is not due to their sudden concern with the health of political parties in our system, but rather is due to a sanction that recently returned after a lengthy hiatus—the ability of the party caucus to take away a committee chairmanship. If one of the goals of the reformers was to improve the degree of party cohesion in government . . . the weakening of the seniority system was a successful reform. Congressional reform has had an effect, and in this one instance it has moved the US legislative process closer to one in which the political parties are not lying prostrate before the thrones of committee chairmen. (225–226)

Members appointed or elected to positions of leadership within the party help to realize the party goals of developing and focusing the legislative agenda, promoting committee accountability, and structuring legislative success. They are the heavy hand of the party. Based on the responsibilities of the leadership team, Members holding positions of party leadership display higher levels of party unity than their colleagues. Even in the less centralized, less-unified Democratically controlled Congress, party leaders evidenced higher levels of party support than their colleagues (Ripley 1967; Peabody 1976; Sinclair 1983). As Loomis (1984) states:

> leaders' party unity scores, as of 1980, ran a bit higher than those of nonleaders. . . . For the most part, leaders appear as slightly party-conscious "middle-men." (193)

Organizational Context

A further factor influencing Members' behavior within the party organization is the organizational context. There are important administrative, purposive, and behavioral differences between the two parties in the contemporary Congress. In terms of structure, they are seemingly quite similar; however, administrative and purposive characteristics of the organization illuminate the severe differences between the Democratic and Republican Parties on the Hill. In terms of administration, the Democratic Caucus has one-quarter the staff and one-tenth of the budget of the Republican Conference. In terms of purpose, the Democratic Caucus serves as an arm of the leadership team to develop responses to Republican legislation, while the Republican Conference operates as a sophisticated public relations firm (Peters 2002). In describing the Conference, Peters notes:

> The Republican Conference operates like a large public relations firm, sponsoring a sophisticated web page (GOP.GOV), organizes large issue conferences, has a major outreach program to talk radio and television shows and other media outlets, has monitored campaign contributions by lobbyists, and has been responsible for specific policy portfolios within the GOP leadership group. The Democratic Caucus functions mostly through a series of issues task forces designed to forge Democratic alternatives to Republican legislation, but has no specific policy portfolio, has a less well developed web site, is not responsible for communications strategy, and is generally subordinate to the floor leader and whip organizations. (2002, 2)

These differences are not only due to majority/minority status, but also are directly associated with party culture. The Republicans' long-standing status as the minority party in Congress prior to 1994 limited their access to positions of power within the institution and resulted in the proliferation of positions within the leadership organization "through which leadership ambition was channeled" (ibid., 17).

The purposes of the two organizations are also different in critical ways. In recent years the Conference has not only streamlined weekly briefings with Member press secretaries, it has also streamlined communication with committees and leadership, and is attempting to streamline communication with the electorate (Peters 2002). Particularly since losing the majority, the Democratic Caucus has become a forum for debate, a patchwork of diversity, and an umbrella for policy-focused task forces. In sum, Peters suggests:

> The Democratic Caucus is coalitional, it works with and through external interest groups, it is subordinated to the committees, and its focus has been more internal than external. The Republican Conference is ideological, it runs on money, it functions more autonomously from the committee system, and its focus is more external than internal. (2002, 33)

At the end of the day, however, an important party-building activity for both parties is internal and external communications. "Party communications services have become a growing activity for building party cohesion" (Forgette 2002, 37). At every level within the organization, communication activities increasingly serve the function of creating a unified message. From the message articulated by the party leaders to the issue briefs circulated by the caucuses, to the order of bill introduction (Forgette 2002), Members are provided with information by the party concerning its priorities and are encouraged to participate in party-building by "staying on message."

Party theory has only recently begun to reflect the diverse party-building activities that contribute to Members' legislative behavior. Partisan activities, such as attending party organizational meetings, promoting the party agenda through internal and external communications and building political capital by assisting with colleagues' campaigns, are important facets of the modern party organization. In the next section, three distinct forms of party-building activity are examined: organizational attendance, national fundraising, and national media appearances to build a more adequate model of women's partisan participation.

Party-Building Activities

There is a hidden element of legislative behavior—that of party building. Members participate in party-building activities to curry favor with colleagues or build "social capital," to use a term now popular in the social sciences (Forgette 2002; for further explication of social capital as a concept, see Coleman 1990; and Putnam 1993). Forgette (2002) suggests:

> Party building activities may not directly affect specific committee action or floor votes; however, these activities may generate greater party identity, informal networks, friendships, and a shared sense of party expectations and destinies among legislative copartisans. Party building activities, in short, maintain and strengthen long-term party success. (5)

This form of activity makes cognitive sense within a number of theoretical frameworks, not only social network theory but also rational choice theory. "Party-building, from (the) rational choice perspective, operates as a means of building reciprocity and information relationships among goal-directed politicians to solve their collective dilemmas" (ibid., 6). Members can have a number of institutional identities, such as an "institutionalist" identity (focused on the committee culture or policy development of the Congress) or a "partisan" identity (focused on the team loyalty or ideological unity of the party) (Connelly and Pitney 1994). We should expect party building activity to differ according to institutional identities (Forgette 2002, 9).

Some have suggested that parties are more election than policy oriented (Cantor and Herrnson 1997). In years past party unity scores have not influenced the distribution of party monies and campaign assistance, and conversely party spending or recruitment has not led to greater party unity (Cantor Herrnson 1997; Clucas 1997). Little research, however, has examined the relationship between party spending and party unity scores since the Republicans have held the majority in the House. This analysis suggests that party culture is an important factor in examining party unity. While campaign spending by the national party organizations might not be related to party unity scores, party-building activities including party fundraising by individual Members should be related to party unity scores or greater ideological loyalty.

As was discussed in the introductory chapter of this book, the Democratic Party illustrates a highly pluralistic structure, whereas the Republican Party illustrates a more elitist structure. Freeman notes:

> Since the Democratic party is composed of groups, the success of individuals whose group identification is highly significant, such as blacks and women, is tied to that of the group as a whole. They succeed as the group succeeds. That is not the case within the Republican party. It officially ignores group characteristics. . . . Generally, individuals succeed insofar as the leaders with whom they are connected succeed. (1986, 336)

For this reason, sponsorship is important in the Republican Party. Incoming freshmen are often "sponsored" by more senior Members within the organization. Sponsors take freshmen Members "under their wings" and "show them the ropes." This practice serves to orient Members to the ethos, protocol, and practices of the party. A number of the prominent women in the Republican Party are sponsored by Republican men (ibid.).

The Republican Party advocates a more unitary conception of representation. Meeting the needs of national interest, such as improving the economy, is the appropriate means for meeting the needs of individual groups. On the other hand, Democrats hold a conception of representation that emphasizes minority coalition-building (ibid.). Freeman states:

> Democrats do not have an integrated conception of a national interest, in part because they do not view themselves as the center of society. The party's components think of themselves as outsiders pounding on the door seeking programs that will facilitate entry into the mainstream. Thus, the party is very responsive to any groups . . . . (ibid., 338)

This ethos is further demonstrated in the organizational style of the two parties. While Democratic Party politics are often characterized as "open" and "confrontational," Republican Party politics are characterized as "closed" and "consensual" (ibid.). The organizational style of the Republican Party most reflects a corporation with discretion located at the top, whereas the organizational style of the Democratic Party is best reflected by a social movement with discretion located among the different vocal groups. The representational ethos and the organizational style of the Democratic Party work hand-in-hand to produce an environment of conflict and change.

One of the major consequences of these attitudinal and structural differences between the parties concerns the role of women within the parties. The Republican Party emphasizes loyalty to the party first and foremost, whereas the Democratic Party provides the vehicle whereby group loyalties may be articulated in the political arena. Freeman (1986) suggests:

> Even in 1976, when Republican feminists were aligned with party leaders, one organizer commented that because the GOP is not "an interest group party . . . the RWTF (Republican Women's Task Force of the National Women's Political Caucus) is viewed with skepticism. Party regulars have a hard time adjusting to the presence of an organized interest." The current leadership views feminist organizations as Democratic party front groups. Thus it is virtually impossible to be both an accepted Republican activist and an outspoken supporter of feminist goals. Since the party discourages people from identifying themselves as members of a group with a group agenda, it minimizes the possibility of multiple loyalties. (348)

Another consequence of the Republican emphasis on party loyalty is wide-spread trust among rank-and-file members of the Republican Party. An emphasis on social and ideological homogeneity fosters a trust of others within the group. Party leaders thus are capable of maintaining discretion over the policy agenda because they benefit from a large degree of member-ship trust (ibid., 351).

In sum, high levels of party unity in the contemporary context could be due to the relative ideological homogeneity of the parties combined with the increased control of party leadership over committees, policy develop-ment, and voting cues. Evidence from the McKinley era suggests that "higher levels of party support . . . were related to the centralized leadership structure and the homogeneity of the constituencies represented by each party" (Brady 1972, 439). In fact, several studies of American legislatures point to these two variables (centralized leadership and constituent homo-geneity) as significant predictors of party support (see MacRae, Jr. 1952; Jewell 1955; Dye 1961; Flinn 1964; Jewell and Patterson 1966, 425; Polsby et al. 1969; Rohde 1991).

What implications does this have for women's legislative behavior? Given the elitist structure of the Republican Party as well as the emphasis on party homogeneity and ideological loyalty, we might expect Republican women, who are more liberal on average than their colleagues on social issues, to have lower party unity scores, and to consequently be underrep-resented in formal positions of power. These women might be underrepre-sented on exclusive committees, among committee and subcommittee chairs, and in the leadership team. In contrast, given the coalitional struc-ture of the Democratic Party, with its emphasis on seniority and diversity, we might expect Democratic women, who are also more liberal on average than their colleagues, to have higher party unity scores yet enjoy at least equal representation in the same formal positions of power.

Nonetheless, academics, journalists, and politicians alike have noted the inability of all women to reach the highest levels of party leadership. Women are often elected to positions of service within the party struc-ture. Since the 104th Congress, the vast majority of Republican Conference Secretaries and Democratic Caucus Secretaries have been women. Some have described it as a token position of power (Peters 2002). Women have not been elected, however, to the most prestigious positions of leadership within the party—until recently. Although her accomplishment is not captured by the data included in this analysis, Rep. Nancy Pelosi (D-CA) was elected to the position of minority whip during the second session of the 107th Congress and to the position of minority leader following the 2002 election. Her victory marks the highest office held by any woman in the House of Representatives. This historic accomplishment was achieved by the Democratic Party, but women have also reached a new height in the Republican Party as well. Deborah Pryce was elected Conference Chair of the Republican Party for the 108th Congress in 2002. While new levels of leadership have been reached lately, these are still the exceptions rather than the rule. Gender theory sheds light on possible reasons for this discrepancy between men and women's status within the party organizations.

Women's Participation

Out of concern about the quality of political representation, gender theory in the legislative context focuses on women's participation in the political discourse of state and national legislatures. Women's inclusion in public debate is important because women bring different *experiences*, *attitudes*, and *resources* to the political table (Schlozman et al. 1995; Tamcrius 1995). Congresswomen are better able to steer feminist policy through the policy process than congressmen because of their interest and desire to affect change for women (Tamerius 1995; see also Thomas 1991). It is possible, however, that women may not be fully effective at promoting feminist policy because of certain gendered power dynamics present in legislative discourse and because of the highly masculinized nature of political talk (Kathlene 1994).

In sex-differentiated group interaction, men and women participate differently. Men are more interested in accomplishing the task at hand, while women are more attentive to maintaining group solidarity (Bales 1950). Men are more likely to offer opinions and guidance and to talk in general (Smith-Lovin and Robinson 1992; see also Eakins 1978; Leet-Pellegrini 1980; Crawford and MacLeod 1990). Conversely, women are more likely to facilitate group discussion, to support the expression of opinions, and to agree with the suggestions of others within the group (Eakins 1978; Ridgeway and Johnson 1990). In the committee setting legislative debate demonstrates gendered group dynamics with men dominating conversation, displaying verbal aggression and interruptive behavior much more than women (Kathlene 1994).

The gendered nature of political institutions and processes also shapes women's participation (Kenney 1997). Political institutions "produce, reproduce and subvert" gender in their processes and arrangements of power (ibid., 456). As such, political settings may reward behavior typically regarded as "male" or "aggressive" and thus magnify insignificant differences in knowledge, interest, and participation.

Across political organizational contexts, gender theorists find that women are limited in their access and effectiveness by gendered discourse regardless of the social composition of the group. "Women, whether they be 10, 20, or 60 percent of an organization, work within the larger confines of gendered institutions and socially prescribed roles" (Kathlene 1995, 167). Female committee chairs use their leadership posts to facilitate dialogue and include more voices at the table while male chairs interject more of their own personal opinions and assert dominant verbal behavior such as cutting off speakers (Kathlene 1994, 572). Female chairs create a more inclusive or facilitating speaking environment while male chairs present a more assertive or challenging speaking environment. In confirmation hearings, women are not given equal access to political debate. Female witnesses before the U.S. Senate Judiciary Committee are given less time to speak, and their testimonies are given less credence. Even those female witnesses who adopt a more masculine linguistic style are treated with less respect than male witnesses (Mattei 1998).

A major concern in this line of research is the impact of the social composition of groups on the "token" individual's behavior (Kanter 1977). Indeed, women hold a minority of leadership roles in most American political institutions. Yet we should be careful to assume that a more "balanced" institutional setting would lead to equal participation. Balanced numbers may not lead to balanced participation. As women's numbers increase, does women's participation in the political debate increase as well? In examining committee behavior, Kathlene (1994) finds support for Yoder's (1991) intrusiveness theory in that "men rather than women became significantly more vocal when women comprised greater proportions of the committee" (179). Whether the gendered contours of political discourse are due to institutional norms rather than gendered norms of behavior *per se* is the subject of some debate.

Women's Status Within the Party Organizations

The number of women in Congress has increased over the last decade for both parties. Table 4.1 illustrates the gender composition of the parties in the House for the 103rd through 107th Congresses. The female composition of the Democratic Party increased from 13.6 percent (35) in the 103rd Congress to 19.8 percent (42) in the 107th Congress.

The dramatic seat gains of the Republican Party throughout the last decade mask the gender compositional change that took place over the same time period. While the female composition of the Republican Party only

Table 4.1   Gender composition of the U.S. House: 103rd to 107th Congresses

	103rd Congress	104th Congress	105th Congress	106th Congress	107th Congress
Democratic men	86.4% 223	85.2% 173	81.6% 168	81.6% 173	80.2% 170
Democratic women	13.6% 35	14.8% 30	18.4% 38	18.4% 39	19.8% 42
Republican men	93.2% 164	92.6% 214	92.5% 211	92.3% 205	91.9% 205
Republican women	6.8% 12	7.4% 17	7.5% 17	7.7% 17	8.1% 18

increased from 6.8 percent in the 103rd Congress to 8.1 percent in the 107th Congress, the actual number of women increased by 50 percent, from 12 to 18.

It is insufficient, however, to just examine the gains women have made in membership. How successful have women been in gaining important leadership roles in the institution? In order to answer this question, this analysis incorporates a novel measure of party leadership. Not only has the leadership structure in the House become increasingly institutionalized over the last century, power has become increasingly centralized in the party apparatus since the committee reforms of the 1970s and the institutional reforms of the Republican Revolution. For these two reasons, it is important to treat party leadership as a group of elected and appointed Members collectively responsible for the electoral and legislative success of the party. The power and prestige that party leadership offers comes at the price of party loyalty and service. Consequently, we should expect that Members inside party leadership should demonstrate higher party unity scores than Members outside of party leadership. The data for this measure was taken from Congressional Quarterly's *Politics in America*, from their list of "Partisan House Committees." When referring to the "leadership team," a dichotomous variable accounts for inclusion in leadership as at least one of the following: the Speaker and floor leaders; the whips, including chief deputy whips, deputy whips, assistant whips, at-large whips, and regional whips; a member of the national campaign committees, a member of the policy committees, and a member of the steering committees. This measure allows us to examine not only women's inclusion in party leadership but also the relationship between party status and voting behavior.

In the Democratic Party, women also made gains in terms of their representation in committees and in leadership (see table 4.2). In the committee

Table 4.2 Distribution of select positions among Democrats by sex

	103rd		104th		105th		106th		107th	
	Male	Female	Male	Female	Male	Female	Male	Female	Male	Female
On exclusive committee	88.6% (62) 27.8%	11.4% (8) 22.9%	90.7% (39) 22.5%	9.3% (4) 13.3%	80.9% (38) 22.6%	19.1% (9) 23.7%	80.9% (38) 22.0%	19.1% (9) 23.1%	80.0% (52) 30.6%	20.0% (13) 31.0%
Committee chair	95.8% (23) 10.3%	4.2% (1) 2.9%	95.0% (19) 11.0%	5.0% (1) 3.3%	100% (19) 11.3%	.0% (0) .0%	95.0% (19) 11.0%	5.0% (1) 2.6%	90.0% (18) 10.6%	10.0% (2) 4.8%
Subcommittee chair	94.5% (103) 46.2%	5.5% (6) 17.1%	90.4% (75) 43.4%	9.6% (8) 26.7%	89.2% (74) 44.0%	10.8% (9) 23.7%	85.2% (69) 39.9%	14.8% (12) 30.8%	84.7% (72) 42.4%	15.3% (13) 31.0%
Leadership	100.0% (5) 2.2%	.0% (0) .0%	83.3% (5) 2.9%	16.7% (1) 3.3%	83.3% (5) 3.0%	16.7% (1) 2.6%	85.7% (6) 3.5%	14.3% (1) 2.6%	83.3% (5) 2.9%	16.7% (1) 2.4%

Whip team	84.9%	15.1%	84.5%	15.5%	77.5%	22.5%	79.5%	20.5%	76.5	23.5%
	(79)	(14)	(71)	(13)	(62)	(18)	(58)	(15)	(13)	(4)
	35.4%	40.0%	41.0%	43.3%	36.9%	47.4%	33.5%	38.5%	7.6%	9.5%
Policy and steering committees	88.2%	11.8%	86.0%	14.0%	78.9%	21.1%	79.5%	20.5%	80.4%	19.6%
	(30)	(4)	(37)	(6)	(30)	(8)	(35)	(9)	(37)	(9)
	13.5%	11.4%	21.4%	20.0%	17.9%	21.1%	20.0%	23.1%	21.8%	21.4%
Campaign committees	87.9%	12.1%	79.1%	20.9%	100.0%	.0%	75.0%	25.0%	50.05%	50.0%
	(29)	(4)	(34)	(9)	(1)	(0)	(3)	(1)	(1)	(1)
	13.0%	11.4%	19.7%	30.0%	.6%	.0%	1.7%	2.6%	.6%	2.4%
Leadership team	85.5%	14.5%	83.1%	16.9%	78.8%	21.2%	79.0%	21.0%	80.0%	20.0%
	(100)	(17)	(98)	(20)	(78)	(21)	(79)	(21)	(44)	(11)
	44.8%	48.6%	56.6%	66.7%	46.4%	55.3%	45.7%	53.8%	25.9%	26.2%

The first row represents the percent of the total population in the group (exclusive committee, committee chair, whip team, and so forth). The second row represents the valid number in the category. The third row represents the total population in the subgroup. In other words, the percentage equals the proportion of the total males or females represented in the group under question.

structure, they enjoyed increased representation on exclusive committees, changing the composition from 11.4 percent female to 20.0 percent female over the respective congresses. They also enjoyed increases as ranking members on subcommittees, more than doubling their numbers from 6 in 1993 to 13 in 2001 and changing the Democratic composition of the group from 5.5 percent to 15.3 percent female. Democratic women were the most underrepresented among full committee chairs, and the gains made across congresses in these positions by women were only modest at best. The number of women who were full committee chairs seemed to fluctuate across congresses. While seemingly increasing from one to two from the 103rd Congress to the 107th Congress, only one woman was a committee chair in the 103rd, 104th, and 106th Congresses, and no women were chairs in the 105th Congress.

In the leadership structure, women made great gains in the Democratic Party. The female composition of the overall leadership team increased from 14.5 percent (17) to 21.0 percent (21) in the 106th Congress. It should be noted that the Democratic leadership reported by *CQ* for the 107th Congress included a much more truncated whip structure than in previous congresses and thus the leadership team variable for this congress possibly underrepresents Democratic women's activities in leadership. These women made great and enduring gains on the policy and steering committees, doubling their representation and increasing the composition from 11.8 percent (4) to 19.6 percent (9) between 1993 and 2001. Democratic women also infiltrated the highest ranks of leadership during the 104th Congress, claiming one of six leadership positions. The composition of the whip team and the campaign committee also seem to have changed to reflect women's increased numbers in Congress, although the data is not complete for all years.

In the Republican Party, women more than doubled if not tripled their numbers on exclusive committees, increasing the female composition of these committees from 4.9 percent (2) to 11.1 percent (7) in the 106th Congress and 8.3 percent (7) in the 107th Congress. They also increased in number as subcommittee chairs. They did not enjoy, however, increases as full committee chairs. In the 105th through 107th Congresses, no Republican women chaired a full committee. They did not make significant gains overall in the leadership structure either. Their representation within the highest ranks of leadership did increase from none in the 103rd Congress to two in the 104th Congress (making the composition of formal leadership 25 percent female), however it remained at this level through the 107th Congress. And their representation within the whip team did increase from four to five from the 103rd to the 104th Congresses, but the overall size of the whip structure also dramatically increased, resulting in a decrease of the female composition of the structure from 22.2 percent to 9.4 percent between these two congresses. Further changes in the 107th Congress reducing the whip structure to its pre-Republican Revolution size decreased the number of Republican women in the group to only two; nonetheless they still constituted 10.5 percent of the membership. They made no advances on the policy and steering committees, decreasing in number from eight in 1993 to four in 2001 and in certain congresses only holding two slots on the committees. Similarly, their numbers shrank on the campaign committee, steadily decreasing from seven in 1993 to two in 2001. Overall, the female composition of the leadership team dropped from 12.0 percent in the 103rd Congress to 7.1 percent in the 107th Congress.

To end here, however, would not paint an adequate picture of women's partisan status in Congress during these years. Although they may not have made tremendous gains in terms of numbers in either the committee structure or the leadership structure during these Congresses, they are proportionately represented in almost every group. Table 4.2 illustrates that the tables have turned in terms of the percentage of men and women holding exclusive committee assignments. In the 103rd Congress, 5 fewer Democratic women enjoyed prestigious committee assignments than Democratic men (27.8% of men versus 22.9% of women). In the 107th Congress, however, a slightly greater percentage of women than men held prestigious assignments (30.6% of men versus 31.0% of women). Both in terms of full committee and subcommittee ranking positions, nonetheless, men have held more than "their fair share" of assignments. While women have not had any more success gaining full committee ranking positions, they have made progress at the subcommittee level. In the 107th Congress, 42.4 percent of Democratic men and 31.0 percent of Democratic women held ranking positions on subcommittees; whereas in the 103rd Congress, 46.2 percent of Democratic men and 17.1 percent of Democratic women held ranking positions on subcommittees.

In the leadership structure as well, Democratic women have enjoyed proportionate assignments with men. A greater percentage of Democratic women than Democratic men have been appointed to the whip team in every Congress included in the analysis. A similar percentage of Democratic women and men have served on the policy and steering committees in every congress in the analysis. A greater percentage of Democratic women than men have served on the campaign committee in every congress since the 104th Congress (except in the 105th where there is insufficient data to make observations). Overall, for most congresses, over half of the women in the Democratic Party served in some sort of leadership capacity, and only once did half of the men in the Democratic Party served in similar capacities (the 104th Congress).

The trend is similar in the Republican Party. Table 4.3 illustrates that for all congresses in which Republicans have held a majority a greater percentage

Table 4.3 Distribution of select positions among Republicans by sex

	103rd Male	103rd Female	104th Male	104th Female	105th Male	105th Female	106th Male	106th Female	107th Male	107th Female
On exclusive committee	95.1% (39) 23.8%	4.9% (2) 16.7%	91.9% (57) 26.6%	8.1% (5) 29.4%	92.4% (61) 28.9%	7.6% (5) 29.4%	88.9% (56) 27.3%	11.1% (7) 41.2%	91.7% (77) 37.6%	8.3% (7) 38.9%
Committee chair	95.7% (22) 13.4%	4.3% (1) 8.3%	90.0% (18) 8.4%	10.0% (2) 11.8%	100.0% (20) 9.5%	.0% (0) .0%	100.0% (20) 9.8%	.0% (0) .0%	100.0% (20) 9.8%	.0% (0) .0%
Subcommittee chair	92.9% (78) 47.6%	7.1% (6) 50.0%	91.7% (77) 36.0%	8.3% (7) 41.2%	90.5% (76) 36.0%	9.5% (8) 47.1%	90.6% (77) 37.6%	9.4% (8) 47.1%	92.2% (83) 40.5%	7.8% (7) 38.9%
Leadership	100.0% (8) 4.9%	.0% (0) .0%	75.0% (6) 2.8%	25.0% (2) 11.8%	75.0% (6) 2.8%	25.0% (2) 11.8%	75.0% (6) 2.9%	25.0% (2) 11.8%	66.7% (4) 2.0%	33.3% (2) 11.1%

Whip team	77.8%	22.2%	90.6%	9.4%	92.4%	7.6%	91.5%	8.5%	89.5%	10.5%
	(14)	(4)	(48)	(5)	(61)	(5)	(54)	(5)	(17)	(2)
	8.5%	33.3%	22.4%	29.4%	28.9%	29.4%	26.3%	29.4%	8.3%	11.1%
Policy and steering committees	86.4%	13.6%	91.2%	8.8%	92.1%	7.9%	95.7%	4.3%	93.2%	6.8%
	(51)	(8)	(31)	(3)	(35)	(3)	(45)	(2)	(55)	(4)
	31.1%	66.7%	14.5%	17.6%	16.6%	17.6%	22.0%	11.8%	26.8%	22.2%
Campaign committees	81.6%	18.4%	81.6%	18.4%	84.2%	15.8%	90.3%	9.7%	93.3%	6.7%
	(31)	(7)	(31)	(7)	(32)	(6)	(28)	(3)	(28)	(2)
	18.9%	58.3%	14.5%	41.2%	15.2%	35.3%	13.7%	17.6%	13.7%	11.1%
Leadership team	88.0%	12.0%	89.2%	10.8%	90.7%	9.3%	92.3%	7.7%	92.9%	7.1%
	(66)	(9)	(83)	(10)	(98)	(11)	(96)	(8)	(79)	(6)
	40.2%	75.0%	38.8%	58.8%	46.6%	58.8%	46.8%	47.1%	38.5%	33.3%

The first row represents the percent of the total population in the group (exclusive committee, committee chair, whip team, and so forth). The second row represents the valid number in the category. The third row represents the total population in the subgroup. In other words, the percentage equals the proportion of the total males or females represented in the group under question.

of Republican women than men held seats on exclusive committees. Similarly, a greater percentage of Republican women than men held ranking positions on subcommittees in every congress except the 107th. In one type of select position, however, Republican women were not so advantaged. A lower percentage of Republican women than men held ranking positions on full committees in every congress except the 104th.

In terms of the leadership structure, a greater percentage of Republican women than men were elected to the highest levels of leadership from the 103rd to the 106th Congresses. In addition, in the 107th Congress, Republican women shared a nearly equivalent proportion of the leadership slots with men. A cursory glance leads us to conclude the Republican women have also had better chances at being elected to the whip team than men. It is important to recognize, however, that the whip team in the Republican party organization grew dramatically in the 104th Congress, while women's numbers on the team remained virtually the same. Women's successes at holding positions on the policy and steering committees have been mixed. Until the 106th Congress, a greater percentage of Republican women than men held positions on these committees. In the 106th Congress, however, the size of the committees grew and the relative representation of women did not. While their numbers decreased on the campaign committee, a greater proportion of Republican women than men held positions on the committee for every congress in the sample except the 107th. Even though the percentage of women on the leadership team as a whole decreased by 42 percent from the 103rd to the 107th Congress, a greater percentage of women than men held positions on the team during every Congress except the 107th.

Since the 103rd Congress, the number of Republican women in Congress has increased by 42 percent, but the general number of Republican women in positions of leadership has remained virtually the same. While it appears that Republican women have not been successful within the party organization, they have enjoyed greater odds than their male colleagues at holding every partisan position except full committee chair. In other words, a greater proportion of Republican women hold positions of party leadership (other than committee chairmanships) than Republican men.

While the gains made by women between the 103rd and 107th Congresses seem modest, a historical look at the leadership positions and committee positions held by women indicate that the 1990s have reached a high point for women in party leadership. The number of women holding positions within party leadership has increased dramatically since the 104th Congress. In contrast to the 81st through 98th Congresses where women in the Democratic Party only held the position of Secretary of the House Democratic Caucus, women in the 107th Congress held an array of positions.

including: Assistant to the House Democratic Leader, Chair of the Democratic Congressional Campaign Committee, House Democratic Whip, Democratic Chief Deputy Whip, House Republican Conference Secretary, and Vice Chair of the House Republican Conference. In both parties, women have made great strides in securing leadership positions.

Gains have been less pronounced in the committee leadership structure. While two female Members served as committee chairs in the 75th through the 77th Congresses, hardly any women have held chairmanships since the 83rd Congress. In fact, only four women have served as committee chairs since the 83rd Congress: Rep. Edith Nourse Rogers (R-MA, 83rd Congress, Chair of Committee on Veterans' Affairs); Rep. Leonor Sullivan (D-MO, 93rd and 94th Congresses, Chair of Committee on Merchant Marine and Fisheries); Rep. Jan Meyers (R-KS, 104th Congress; Chair of Committee on Small Business); and Rep. Nancy Johnson (R-CT, 104th Congress, Chair of Committee on Standards of Official Conduct). While women have had some recent success in attaining party leadership positions, they have had very little success in attaining committee chairmanships. Now that we have examined women's general representation in the committee structure and the party structure, we are ready to examine women's actual participation in and evaluations of the party organizations.

Women's Support of the Party Organizations

Chapter 3 illustrated that Democratic women illustrate significantly higher party unity scores than Democratic men. Contrastingly, Republican women have significantly lower party unity scores than their male colleagues. It is important to realize, however, that this is only one form of party support. It is the most basic measure of party support. There are other ways in which Members demonstrate support for their party organization. In particular, two venues in the modern congressional era have become popular outlets for Members to participate in party-building activities: the establishment of leadership PACs and participation in national political media.

Women's Participation in Party-Building Activities

Analyzing party support scores does little to tell us about the active support given by Members to both the official and political wings of the two parties. While measuring support scores might reveal whether there are discrepancies between male and female partisan voting patterns, it does not reveal the extent to which men and women are partisan actors on the political scene. Do women attend organizational meetings to the same degree that men do? Do women participate in the same kind of fundraising activities as men? Are they as successful in raising funds as men? Do they act as public spokespersons for the party through the venue of national media? Do they view their role(s) in the party in the same way that men do, or are there critical differences that might illuminate the way that gender and partisanship interact to mold congressional behavior? These are the kinds of questions explored in this analysis of women's participation in party-building activities. This level of analysis yields profitable findings that take us further than previous studies built on party support scores.

In chapter 3, we established that Republican women do not support the party through their voting behavior to the same degree as their male colleagues. We might expect then that Republican women would not participate in other party-building activities to the same degree as men either. We have already discovered, however, that women are proportionally represented throughout the leadership structure except at the very highest level. Is this because they support the party through means other than voting? The main question driving this analysis is whether or not women illustrate different patterns of party support from men through their organizational behavior. Three forms of party-building activities are examined: organizational attendance, national fundraising, and media participation.

Organizational Attendance

Do women attend organizational meetings more or less on average, than men? Or are there other factors that predict Member organizational support independent of gender? Data from the organizational records of the Republican Party sheds light on this type of party-building activity. Unfortunately, attendance records could not be obtained from the Democratic Caucus. It should be noted, however, that the party-building activities of Republican women are more crucial to the argument of this study given the electoral cross-pressures these women face, their more liberal ideology scores, and their lower party unity scores.

Even though there were a few critical events that possibly affected turnout at the conference meetings, for the most part attendance was rather stable across the first session of the 107th Congress. Members were never in total attendance (there were 222 Republican Members in the House during the first session of the 107th Congress). On a few occasions, however, attendance reached 85 percent.

It appears that there is no significant difference between the participation rates of men and women in the Republican Party (see table 4.4).

Table 4.4   Conference attendance by sex

Sex	Mean	N	s. d.
Men	.6355	208	.2656
Women	.6895	18	.2096
Total	.6398	226	.261

The dataset is based on attendance records from 39 Republican Conference meetings. For the most part, these conference meetings were part of the routine weekly meeting schedule. The House Republican Conference, under the leadership of Chairman J.C. Watts, Jr., held its meetings on Wednesdays at 10:00 a.m. when the House was in legislative session. On occasion, special conferences are called to discuss legislative strategy or to provide necessary emergency information to the membership.

Note that the number of cases is greater than the total number of Republican Members in the House during the first session of the 107th Congress. During this session, a small number of Members either died in office or retired before the fulfillment of their term. In order to fully capture the participation rates of every Member of Conference, the records of both these Members and the Members elected to replace them are included in the analysis. Their attendance rates were individually adjusted to reflect the proportion of meetings they attended out of the total possible meetings they could have attended. The only other included case not explained by simple replacement is the addition of Rep. Randy Forbes (VA-4) to the Republican Conference after the death of Rep. Norman Sisisky, the Democrat previously representing this district.

Republican men, on average, attended conference meetings 64 percent of the time. Surprisingly, Republican women attended conference meetings 68 percent of the time. At the highest level of official party organizational activity, men and women appear to attend meetings at equal rates.

It should be noted, however, that the standard deviation for men's attendance rates is six percent larger than the standard deviation for women's attendance rates (see table 4.4). This is noteworthy because it is contrary to what we might expect. We would expect that the standard deviation for the women would be larger than for the men because the size of the group is so much smaller. There were only 18 women as opposed to 208 men in the Republican Conference during the first session of the 107th Congress. What this suggests is that while men and women on average attend conferences at fairly equal rates, the distributions are different in these two groups. The distribution is wider among men than it is among women suggesting that the average for women more accurately describes the attendance pattern of the group than the average for men. In other words, there is more variance in male attendance rates than there is in female attendance rates.

Fundraising
Recent developments in gender theory within the context of campaigns and elections suggest that gender is not a significant factor in predicting a

Member's ability to raise campaign funds. Until women increase their numbers in Congress, however, the majority of female candidates will run as challengers and will lack the institutional resources (such as incumbency, ranking positions, and credit-claiming) available to most male candidates. It is important to note the implications of the pervasive myth that women are inferior fundraisers. Uhlaner and Schlozman (1986) suggest that we should recognize the "potential potency of that belief" (46). They suggest:

> If political influentials believe that women cannot raise money, they will be reluctant to encourage women to become candidates. If potential women contenders believe that they will have trouble filling their campaign coffers, they will hesitate to run. Therefore, the assumption that women candidates are disadvantaged with respect to campaign finance has potential political consequences regardless of its veracity. (ibid.)

It is true that this myth is held even among the political elite. In my interviews, however, only Democratic female Members mentioned the trouble women have raising campaign funds, during interviews. In evaluating the strengths of a female colleague, one Democratic female Member stated:

> Pelosi (D-CA) can raise lots of money . . . which is a huge issue for women. Traditionally, they (female candidates) are seen as not as strong. I'm not sure if this is true person to person. But because of their socialization, it's harder for them to ask for help.

Republican women in general painted a different picture of their ability to raise campaign funds. One female Republican Member noted:

> Do you know that (Member X) and I were first and second in fundraising in our class. There's a myth that women can't raise money. That's not true anymore. I used to be a (Profession X) and discussed money all the time . . . so it doesn't bother me. (Member X) is very well organized as well.

Similarly, when asked how she personally viewed her role in the party, another female Republican Member commented: "I could help a whole lot more than I do. I am very good at campaigns. I have a lot of discipline." From this comment, it appears that not only do some more junior women not feel disadvantaged in raising campaign funds, they actually feel skilled at campaigning including fundraising and think they have something to offer the party in that area.

In recent years, the establishment of leadership PACs has become a popular party-building activity. These PACs represent a distinct form of party-building activity (that of fundraising) that has become crucial to understanding legislative behavior in the modern Congress. Leadership PACs are technically created to provide fundraising money to colleagues' campaigns, but in reality they serve as political favors and help the Member achieve clout in the party. For example, Members with leadership PACs have better odds at securing ranking positions on committees than other Members (Center for Responsive Government). For this reason, it is important for us to understand who has leadership PACs.

In the 107th Congress, forty-two Democratic Members were affiliated with leadership PACs, while only seven Democratic Members held the highest-ranking partisan leadership posts. Nearly 40 percent more Republican Members (64) were affiliated with leadership PACs in 2001 than Democratic Members in the same year, while only eight Republican Members held the highest-ranking partisan leadership posts. Granted, 83.3 percent of Democratic party leaders and 62.5 percent of Republican party leaders had leadership PACs, but 96 leadership PACs were affiliated with Members outside of the inner circle of party leadership.

Overall, women in both parties are just as likely to be associated with a leadership PAC as their male colleagues. If we examine the distribution of leadership PACs by party and gender, however, we discover clear differences between Republicans and Democrats (see table 4.5). A smaller percentage of Democratic Members have established leadership PACs than Republicans Members. Proportionately speaking, female Democrats have the fewest leadership PACs. Only 2.60 percent of female Democratic Members were affiliated with leadership PACs in the 103rd Congress. While the percentage of Democratic women with leadership PACs has steadily grown, this group still has the fewest PACs of any group. In stark contrast (proportionately speaking), female Republicans Members have the most leadership PACs. Nearly 36 percent of Republican women were affiliated with leadership PACs in the 106th Congress, and in the 107th Congress twice the percentage of Republican women were affiliated with leadership PACs than the percentage of Democratic women.

Media

A third form of party-building activity that has become increasingly popular in the modern Congress is media participation. Communications both inside and outside the party organization have become important venues for the collection, articulation, and dissemination of partisan information. One way in which Members act as spokespersons for the party or communicate the party message is through participation on nationally televised political talk shows.

Table 4.5 Leadership PACs by sex: 105th to 107th Congresses

	105th	106th	107th
Male Democrats			
% with Leadership PACs	10.10	15.03	20.00
Number with LPACs	17	26	34
s. d.	.3025	.3584	.4012
Valid *N*	168	173	170
Female Democrats			
% with Leadership PACs	2.60	10.36	19.00
Number with LPACs	1	4	8
s. d.	.1622	.3074	.3974
Valid *N*	38	39	42
Male Republicans			
% with Leadership PACs	16.60	23.90	28.80
Number with LPACs	35	49	59
s. d.	.3729	.4275	.4539
Valid *N*	211	205	205
Female Republicans			
% with Leadership PACs	17.60	35.29	27.80
Number with LPACs	3	6	5
s. d.	.3930	.4926	.4610
Valid *N*	17	17	18

The data for this analysis was only available from the 1998 election cycle forward through http://www.opensecrets.org. Referencing the Federal Election Commission only provided filing information on individual leadership PACs since the 2000 election cycle. Consequently, the table includes only the 105th through the 107th Congresses.

While party leadership theory to date has only suggested that party leaders participate in media, in reality a large number of Members take part in this activity. In 2000 during the second session of the 106th Congress, sixty-six Democratic Members and seventy-one Republican Members made at least one appearance on the political talk shows included in this analysis. These numbers increased in the first session of the 107th Congress, with seventy-one Democratic Members and eighty-six Republican Members making at least one appearance. In fact, some of the most frequent television guests held no position of formal leadership within the party. Just as women equal men in the establishment of leadership PACs, so women of both parties participate at equal levels in this form of party-building activity (see table 4.6).

Table 4.6   Media appearances by party and sex in 2000 and 2001

	Democrats				Republicans			
	2000		2001		2000		2001	
	Males	Females	Males	Females	Males	Females	Males	Females
Mean number of appearances	2.041 (5.818)*	1.615 (2.917)	1.377 (3.223)	1.500 (2.873)	2.566 (6.938)	2.647 (6.422)	1.956 (5.228)	0.889 (1.530)
Maximum number of appearances	45	14	22	10	47	24	33	5
% Participating	28.90	41.0	33.5	33.3	30.2	52.9	39.0	33.3
Number participating	50	16	57	14	62	9	80	6
Valid N	173	39	170	42	205	17	205	18

* Standard deviations in parentheses.

On average, both Republicans and Democrats participate at equal levels in media. Approximately 36.1 percent of Members appeared at least once on a nationally televised political talk show in 2001 (33.5% of Democrats and 38.6% of Republicans). Perhaps this is due to the tendency of media outlets to interview both sides of the aisle in the spirit of objective journalism. In general, however, more Republican Members participate in media than Democratic Members. In terms of women's participation, a larger percentage of women (in both parties) participated in media than men in 2000. Surprisingly, a higher percentage of Republican women (52.9%) than Democratic women (41%) appeared on nationally televised political talk shows in 2000. Female Democrats averaged the fewest number of appearances (1.62), whereas female Republicans averaged the most number of appearances (2.65). In contrast, however, a smaller proportion of women in both parties than men participated in media in 2001. While 33.5 percent of Democratic men appeared on talk show in 2001, 33.3 percent of Democratic women did. And while 39.0 percent of Republican men appeared on talk shows in 2001, 33.3 percent of Republican women did. In terms of the average number of appearances of women on political talk shows in 2001, Democratic women remained fairly constant, appearing an average of 1.5 times. Republican women's appearances, on the other hand severely diminished, dropping from 2.65 times on average in 2000 to 0.89 times in 2001.

Several speculations can be drawn concerning why Republican women were not so involved in the media in 2001. One apparent factor is the declining participation of Rep. Ileana Ros-Lehtinen, who in 2000 repeatedly appeared on talk shows to discuss the Elian Gonzalez issue. Further, the agenda markedly shifted in 2001 from a domestic policy agenda emphasizing education, social security, and prescription drugs to a foreign policy agenda centered on the War on Terror. Because the data source does not suggest the subject matter of the guest appearances, we are left to draw our own conclusions on this decrease in Member participation.

After considering popular forms of party-building activity in the modern Congress, we are left to ask how these forms of partisan support correspond with party support through legislative voting behavior. Among Democratic Members, electoral marginality was significantly associated with affiliation with a leadership PAC in 2000. Marginal Democratic Members were significantly less likely to be affiliated with a leadership PAC than secure Democratic Members. This relationship is what we might expect. We would expect that marginal Members would have less time to devote to party-building activities, particularly those involving extra fundraising. Also significantly associated with leadership PACs is party leadership. Those Members who are part of the Democratic leadership team are also more likely to be affiliated with a leadership PAC. Finally, Members affiliated with a leadership PAC were also more likely to participate in media in 2000.

Among Republican Members, we see both similar and different patterns. Members who were a part of the leadership team were also likely to be affiliated with a leadership PAC. Members who participate in media additionally were more likely to be affiliated with a leadership PAC. In contrast to the pattern among Democrats, however, electoral marginality was not significantly associated with affiliation with a leadership PAC. In other words, electorally marginal Members were just as likely to have leadership PACs as electorally secure Members.

When we examine these correlations by partisanship and gender, we find generally the same patterns. Among Democratic men in 2000, association with a leadership PAC was associated with media participation and being part of the leadership team. Similarly, among Democratic women, media participation was also associated with affiliation with a leadership PAC. Interestingly, electoral marginality was significantly and negatively correlated with membership on the leadership team. This indicates that women who were part of the leadership structure were also significantly more electorally secure than those women who were not part of the leadership structure.

Among Republican males, affiliation with a leadership PAC was significantly and positively associated with both media participation and membership on the party leadership team in both 2000 and 2001. Among Republican females, however, none of the partisan activities were significantly associated in either year. It is possible that these associations do not reach statistical significance because of the limited number of observable cases.

The above analysis indicates that there are significant associations among the party-building activities measured for this study. Factor Analysis was conducted for purposes of data reduction. Given the significant associations found among party-building activities in the correlation matrix, a series of variables were examined using factor analysis to test the stability of the component created from the three variables of interest—association with a leadership PAC, holding a formal leadership position, and media appearances. Employing an eigenvalue cut-point of 1.0, a single component was drawn from the three variables. This single component was included as a variable in the regression models to measure the party-building activity of Members. The principal component analysis explains about 43.574 percent of the total variance in these three variables. The factor constructed collapses these party-building activities onto a single dimension and allows for less biased estimates.

A regression model was estimated to understand the relationship between party building activities and voting behavior in 2000 and 2001. While generally the model does not explain much variance in party support, estimation of the predictive model yields significant differences between the two parties (see table 4.7). Among Democrats, female Members are significantly more unified with the party than male Members (significant at the $p < .01$ level in 2000 and at the $p < .001$ level in 2001). Electorally secure Members are also more unified with the party than marginal Members (significant at the $p < .05$ level in 2000 and at the $p < .001$ level in 2001). Finally, those Members who are involved in party-building activities are also significantly more unified with the party than Members who are not involved in these activities (significant at the $p < .05$ level in both years).

Among Republicans, we see a different pattern. The relationship between female Republican Members and party unity scores is also significant, but the relationship is in the opposite direction. Republican women, as we might expect from the previous chapters, are significantly less unified with the party than their male colleagues (significant at the $p < .001$ level in 2000 and at the $p < .01$ level in 2001). In contrast to the Democratic model, seniority is also associated with party unity, with more senior Members demonstrating lower party unity scores than less senior Members (significant at the $p < .01$ level in both years). While electoral marginality is significantly associated with Democratic Members' party unity scores, it is not nearly as significantly associated with Republican Members' party unity scores when taking into consideration party-building activities. This variable is only significantly associated with party unity scores in 2001 and only at the $p < .05$ level. In other words, marginal Republicans demonstrate more similar patterns of voting behavior to their secure partisan colleagues than marginal Democrats.

108

Table 4.7 Predicting party unity by party in 2000 and 2001

| | 2000 | | 2001 | |
	Democrats b (s.e.)	Republicans b (s.e.)	Democrats b (s.e.)	Republicans b (s.e.)
Constant	86.632 (1.602)	92.907 (.983)	87.966 (1.629)	95.779 (.677)
Female	6.042 (2.084)**	−6.456 (1.852)***	8.100 (2.098)***	−4.130 (1.342)**
Seniority	.021 (.105)	−.220 (.074)**	−.160 (.112)	−.151 (.055)**
Electoral marginality	−3.538 (1.795)*	−1.042 (1.146)	−9.343 (2.004)***	−1.752 (.809)*
Party-building activities	1.780 (.854)*	1.112 (.506)*	1.968 (.955)*	.688 (.379)
Female party-building activities	−.634 (2.553)	4.478(2.022)*	−2.229 (1.953)	3.002 (1.438)*
Adj. R^2	.063 (11.4180)	.101 (7.2241)	.163 (11.8511)	.102 (5.4028)
Durbin–Watson	1.907	1.564	1.881	2.140

*p <.05 level
**p <.01 level
***p <.001 level

Party-building activities are significantly and positively associated with party unity scores but only in 2000. Republican Members who participate in party-building activities also illustrate more party unity in their voting behavior (significant at the $p < .05$ level). Why is this relationship not present in 2001? The theoretical framework of this study suggests that Republicans in general are more ideologically homogenous than Democrats. Perhaps party-building activities are not as strong a predictor of Republican voting behavior because there is not much variance in their voting behavior with which to begin.

The most important relationship for purposes of the present analysis, however, involved the significant association between female Members' participation in party-building activities and party unity scores. Female Republicans who participate in partisan activities are significantly more unified in their voting behavior with the party than either their female copartisan colleagues who do not participate or their male copartisan colleagues who do participate in the same activities (significant at the $p < .05$ level in both years).

Two conclusions can be deduced from these findings. First, it appears that Members of Congress participate as partisans to varying degrees. Second, there appear to be no gendered patterns in party-building activities. Both men and women attend party organizational meetings, participate in party fundraising, and participate in national media. When looking at the connection between party-building activities and party-line voting, it appears that for both parties there is a significant connection. Particularly among Republican women, those women who participate in some forms of party-building activities are also more likely to offer party support through their voting behavior. It makes sense that Republican women who are electorally secure enough to invest time in national fundraising activities are also more able to vote with the party. From here we turn to the Members themselves for an understanding of women's perceptions of the party organizations. By looking at the parties through the eyes of the Members, we develop a much clearer picture of the unique and gendered organizational environment in which women participate as partisans.

Women's Evaluations of the Party Organizations

In evaluating the contribution of the parties on the Hill, most every Member interviewed noted the camaraderie facilitated by the party organizations.

The parties offer Members the opportunity to interact with those who share their philosophy and interests. A Republican female Member noted that the party offered her the

> opportunity to get to know colleagues. It offers a base idea from which to move an idea. I've always liked to think of them as a "committees without an issue." It's an opportunity to find those of like mind.

Similarly, a Democratic female Member stated:

> I value the ability to network . . . to develop relationships where you learn more about the needs and interests of the people in your state. I value the chance to talk to someone with a shared agenda or views. The Caucus does believe that government has a role. I value working with people who have a shared basic philosophy.

Yet the observations made by Members regarding what they value about the party organizations also clearly reflected the distinct party ethos described throughout the party culture literature. Several of the observations offered by female Members reflected the findings of the party culture literature concerning the Republican and Democratic party organizations. Republican women, when asked what they valued about the party organization pointed to the party unity promoted by the Conference, and the ability to get things done. One female Republican Member noted:

> You have to have organization to get things done. I am very proud of the party. We have stood together on rules and process. We have to stand together to be effective. I've also been impressed with leadership. Hastert is a very caring person. J.C. Watts is very sincere. You don't see partisanship like that very often—caring about people.

Similarly, another female Member commented, "I like (the Conference) being able to drive priorities such as health care." Yet another stated, "The party offers leadership on these (priority) issues. It provides a basic philosophy." Another remarked:

> The camaraderie and support. The party makes it possible for us to get a lot done. I also appreciate the information provided by the party. I appreciate the opportunity for briefings. It's a chance for educating myself and taking it back home to my constituents. It also gives me the opportunity to become close to people in leadership who are the changers.

Still another female Member expressed that she valued the party for:

> the information on issues. The Conference serves to rally the troops . . . to provide unity. The meetings emphasize where we are alike and that's useful.

We can air both sides of issues without it becoming a public issue. It gives us
a chance to hear from the Speaker who most specifically gives us a sense of
where the other branches are going. It gives us a feel for the executive branch.

One junior Republican female Member noted that this characteristic of the
Republican party culture was useful in the contemporary context given the
narrow seat margin of partisan control in the House, stating: "They (party
leadership) help keep the majority."

Just as Republican women reflected through their comments the ethos
of the Republican Party, several of the observations offered to me by female
Democratic Members reiterated the ethos of the Democratic Party as promoting diversity, coalition-building, and equality. For some, it was exactly
this ethos that led to their identification with the Democratic Party. One
particular female Member commented:

> I had a Republican mother and a Democratic father. I come from a moder-
> ate gypsy-moth background. I valued the diversity of the Democratic Party at
> a young age. I felt like I would hear from a larger cross-section of society.

Several female Members noted that they valued not only the ability to
express their point of view, but also the ability to hear the opinions of their
colleagues. One female Democratic Member stated: "We get an opportunity to put our point of view out there. Being that there are so many
Members from all across the country, it is valuable to hear other points of
view." Still another expressed that she valued the camaraderie offered by the
party organization, elaborating:

> I value the ability to hear what my colleagues feel about certain issues. In a
> positive way, I'm amazed at the diversity in color, gender, and opinions. The
> Democratic Party truly reflects the American people. It's a wonderful micro-
> cosm of the great American dream.

While all of the Democrats interviewed agreed with the party ethos of open
dialogue, some articulated the consequences of this ethos for party unity.
One female Member explained:

> It (the party organization) provides the opportunity to hear a diversity of
> views. It is frustrating, however, that we don't vote lock step. But on diversity,
> I value the ability to stand up and speak my mind. I'm really proud to be a
> member of a disorganized party. With more organization, we could possibly
> get more done, but I'm more for individuality.

Women's Perceived Roles in the Party Organizations

During interviews, Members were asked to evaluate their personal role in the party organizations on the Hill. The responses to this question provide valuable insight into both the participation of women and the status of women within the party organizations.

Three specific roles were clearly defined by female Republican Members. Some Members thought that what they had to offer the party was expertise at the electoral level. One Member, though limited in her participation, suggested: "I could help a whole lot more than I do. I am very good at campaigns. I have a lot of discipline." Another Member articulated a similar role, stating: "I see my role as that of a motivator more than anything else. I try to get people involved at grassroots level. I'm good at getting out the message, getting out the vote."

Others, in evaluating their role within the party, pointed to their position within the state delegation as trailblazers. One such female Republican Member noted: "I'm somewhat of a pioneer. I'm the only Republican woman in the (State X) delegation. I'm one of too few women." Another expressed that she saw herself not only as a pioneer in her state delegation, but also as a pioneer on her committee. She stated:

> I am the first Republican female ever elected to Congress in the state of (X). I see myself primarily as a role model for my district. I don't do national things so much. I am the only Republican female with a (issue X) voice. I sit on the (X) Committee and am out front on those issues.

Some female Republican Members acknowledged the ideological difference between them and their male colleagues. They felt that their role in the party was to facilitate ideological compromise. One female Member said, "I see my role as building consensus as a moderate." Another reflected:

> How many Republican women are there? Only 18? Geez that's not very many. I see myself as a more flexible, more moderate Member on some issues. I'm a "floating kind of Member." My identification doesn't necessarily determine my vote. I see women in general as a broadening aspect to the party. I campaigned as a "new face at the table."

Still another remarked: "I don't think about party politics as such. . . . I don't think about my role in the party. I think it hurts on a national level to think that way. We don't work together like we should."

A few female Republican Members suggested that they don't view themselves as having a particular role in the party. One simply stated, "I never thought of myself as having a role specifically as a Republican." More often, however, female Republican Members viewed their role within the party organization as limited. A junior Member reflected:

> I'm probably not as successful as I would like to be. I'm not as much a part of things as I used to be in other things. I have wonderful committee assignments. I appreciate being able to take on a position on the Speaker's (Issue X) Task Force. . . . I was actually blocked from leadership because (omitted to protect the identity of the Member).

While some did not blatantly suggest that their roles were limited, they did elude to it in their comments. One noted: "I see myself as a supporting player. It's hard to be, but you have to do your time." A freshman female Republican Member, while recognizing her limited role, suggested the importance of the representation of women within party leadership, stating: "My role is to really learn as a freshman. I don't see myself as a leader. Women have a different perspective, and need to get to leadership." Only one female Member that I interviewed, however, saw herself having a leadership role. She stated:

> I see myself as a spokesman for the party among women for Republican principles. I feel a great responsibility for doing media. There are not enough women who do it. It's hard work. I'm a leader on some issues such as the (Issue X).

In this brief description, she illuminated a number of informal modes of leadership unaccounted for by formal measures. First, she suggested that an important leadership function she served involved communications, particularly through media outlets. Second, she suggested that her role included leadership on specific issues.

In contrast, Democratic women communicated not only definite roles within the party organization, but also inclusion within leadership. A few of these women noted the importance of their gender to their partisan role(s). One remarked:

> I speak up through my role as the Democratic Women's Caucus liaison to leadership, which is separate from the Women's Caucus. But my focus continues to be with my district.

Gender not only affects these women's roles at the national level, but also within their state delegations and within their districts. Another

Democratic female Member noted:

> I was in leadership in the (State X) House. I was the only woman some of the time. Right now, I am the second woman to be elected to the House. There hasn't been another since 1958. My role is very different than I had previously envisioned. I'm a congressional leader and a leader for women. I'm the highest elected woman in the state. So it's important that I be there for political Caucus events, as a party leader in the 4th congressional district. I take my role working on campaigns very seriously as did my predecessor for me. I have a role here, attending more Task Forces built on issues with a broad cross-section of coalitions.

As this Member suggested, some women described their role in the party as being an issue expert. They participate as liaisons, on task forces, and in committee rooms. One Member stated:

> As a physician, they (leadership) think I'm kind of an expert (on health issues). I've always tried to be active. . . . Compared to others, they've found me to be very supportive. They see me as a leader in healthcare . . . as someone they can depend on.

Another expressed:

> It varies on the issues. I'm perceived by the elective leadership as a resource on technological issues. They are my constituents' issues. I get along with all of the elements of the party, the Blue Dogs and the Progressives.

None of the women I interviewed indicated that they felt excluded from leadership. A number even described their role as being a team player and a leader among their colleagues. An African American female Member explained:

> I see my role as being the "stellar ideal . . . but most respectful." I see myself as loyal but slightly independent . . . not quite a party activist. I'm fortunate enough to sit at the leadership table. I was elected the leader of my class. I vote majority Democrat. I'm a team player. I'm probably not as partisan as some, but certainly one they (leadership) can come to.

Another female Member reiterated: "In Congress, I aspire to be a good team player and a leader among my classmates. I am the president of the sophomore class. At home, I'm a leader in the party."

Perceived Gender Differences Within
the Party Organization

In evaluating their similarities and differences with their male co-partisans, female Members also illuminated party-based gender differences. Republican women, by and large, noted the similarities between them and their male colleagues. Any differences were noted as a side-note to the general reflection of sameness. Democratic women, on the other hand, commented on the gender differences between them and their male colleagues.

The majority of female Republican Members interviewed noted the similarities between them and their male colleagues. One Member simply stated, "I really don't see them as any different." A few noted ideological differences, but interestingly these differences were in both directions. A conservative female commented:

> I don't see myself as different from my Republican male colleagues. Some see themselves as moderate, so we may not vote the same . . . but in general I think we're all the same.

A more liberal female Member, on the other hand, noted, "I don't really see that much difference. I'm different from some, but not overall. Some are much more partisan, but not all."

Another group of female Republican Members, although noting the overriding philosophical similarities, suggested the emphasis they personally place on family and their children. For instance, one freshman female Member expressed:

> I think fundamentally there is no difference at all. I know best my fellow freshman. We're all excited about being here and charged up. We haven't developed any cynicism. At heart, I share similarities with men who are very family-oriented; I gravitate towards men who will share about their kids and are very grounded in their homes. Philosophically we are the same. We both believe in less government, more local control, lower taxes, and strong fiscal restraint and the military. Everything gets so personal with me that I forget the big issues.

Similarly, a more junior female Member noted the added familial responsibilities faced by women:

> We are similar in our ideology, our philosophy . . . in almost all ways. The only difference is the amount of juggling that women have to do. Men have it fairly easy. We are the nurturers and the caretakers.

A few women more clearly articulated the ways in which they differ from their male colleagues. For some, their gender contours the way in which they approach their job. One Member stated:

> Sue Kelly, Sue Myrick, Kay Granger . . . we take a systems approach to legislating. We are concerned with other points of view. We are in the business of policy-making. The men get more involved in lines of right and wrong.

Another Member similarly expressed:

> We are quite similar. Dave Camp said, "(Member X), you vote policy rather than politics." I never wanted the job. . . . I only ran to keep the seat in Republican hands. I have no urgent need. The job doesn't give me a big ego boost. I just like trying to solve problems. I mean there are the normal male/female differences. I am pro-life, but I don't like when men get on a high-horse with no clue about what it feels like. Men look at issues from a numbers perspective. Females have a people perspective. Women do react to things in a much more emotional or immediate way than do men.

Another stated:

> Most women are conscientious and they like to complete jobs. Women don't make promises, claim victories, or give facts that are incorrect. Men posture a lot. J.C. is different. He is low key . . . high quality. We are very similar in our set of beliefs, however. We believe in the power of the individual to help the person next door. If you create a reliance on government that the Democrats want to do, we won't move forward.

Still another framed it this way:

> I'm similar to them on a lot of positions I take. I'm a standard Republican who believes in free market. We're different in terms of issues at the top of my list. . . . I'm also more likely to look at other less clean cut issues. . . . I think outside the traditional Republican box.

The differences noted by female Republican Members extended beyond the way in which they approach the job of policymaking. One female Member shared with me her personal experience in the more informal network of the party organization. She reflected:

> It seems that my male colleagues live with a sense of entitlement. Informal relationships are just as important (as formal relationships). They have a camaraderie. They also have the support of a wife. When we as Members go

on trips or CODELS, the men get briefed and the women go shopping. If my husband goes with me, what can he do? The women always want to surround me and show me pictures of their grandchildren. The men gather and talk about defense. I want to be over there talking about defense!

A real emphasis on diversity pervaded all of the comments given to me by Democratic female Members. For example, one Member reflected:

> They are all so different. Men who have been here for 40 years behave a certain way. The youngsters coming along behave a different way. On both sides, you have hard working people. Members show up every week, have long days and long hours, and then go home and do the same thing in the district.

Similarly, another female Democratic Member stated:

> Especially in (State X), I'm different in the fact that I'm the congresswoman from (State X), not from the 4th district. People from the state always come over to see me. The guys tease me about being "the little sister in the delegation." Of course, it's with a lot of respect. Otherwise I see us as similar . . . whether male or female, we are all different—and yet we are all the same.

Compared to Republican women, however, Democratic women by and large focused on the differences between them and their male copartisan colleagues rather than the similarities. These gender differences were also largely reflective of the differences previously noted in the congressional literature.

Some Democratic women noted the important differences in the way men and women approach problems. One stated:

> They are the guys I hang out with. . . . There is a difference in the way women and men see things. We see things totally. . . . We look at the whole sphere. We see things holistically . . . round. Men see an object and go straight to it and forget about all those affected. It's not at all an issue of politics.

These differences involve not only women's approach to problems, but also the issues important to women as opposed to men. A black female Member observed:

> Some of them aren't as sensitive to issues important to minorities as I would like for them to be . . . seeing how that connects to the nation's healthcare as a whole. They get tired of me talking about the same issue, and don't see it as important.

Other women focused on the more behavioral differences between them and their male co-partisan colleagues. Some noted differences in the organizational behavior of men and women. One Democratic female Member, when asked about the similarities and differences between male and female Democratic Members, remarked, "It's hard to know. . . . I've never been a man. Men aren't necessarily more ambitious people, just different in their interest in leadership."

A few women actually noted differences in the way in which they and their male colleagues communicate or interact in the organizational setting. One black female Democratic Member stated:

> Gender is a factor that allows me to have the advantage of heightened sensitivity to certain things. I don't have the burden of trying to prove my strength by yelling. I can listen. Being a woman allows me to feel and act without embarrassment of being perceived as weak . . . and that's a strength. I have certain liberties that gender and age give me. I'm not intimidated by certain things. As a mother and a grandmother, I know how dependent men can be, and yet how stern they can be. These men are no different. Any woman can use her gender to her advantage. Laws should have a sense of feeling. Depth can be used to your advantage. We can communicate.

Similarly, another female Member remarked:

> They are also a diverse group. Some of them are conservative, and some are wild-eyed liberals. You can't tell outside looking in who's faking it and who knows what they're talking about. My testosterone level is certainly lower! (Laughs) . . . I don't think I get my ego so involved. I'm more focused on substantive outcomes. Men on both sides of the aisle are like that.

Conclusion

There are several ways to measure women's representation within the party organization. In terms of sheer numbers, women are sorely underrepresented as a group. While women comprise 50 percent of the population, they comprise only 16 percent of the Congress. In terms of status within the Congress, however, women are generally advantaged. More women than men have the opportunity to hold the prestigious positions of the committee and leadership structures. Nonetheless, women are not even proportionately represented in the highest levels of leadership. They are noticeably absent among full committee chairs and formal elected leadership. This has been the case for both parties until recently.

Within the party organizations, women perceive the party apparatus, their role within the party, and their relative behavior differently. Republican women applaud the ethos of the Republican party organization for its emphasis on unity and leadership. Democratic women, on the other hand, applaud the ethos of the Democratic party organization for its emphasis on diversity and open dialogue.

Republican women see their role within the party organization as under-developed and limited to a supportive role. Democratic women, conversely, see their role within the party as clearly defined and instrumental. Democratic women see their voice as affecting leadership, whereas Republican women see their role as following leadership.

Republican women also view their personal behavior as quite similar to that of their male colleagues. Contrastingly, Democratic women see their behavior as quite different from that of their male copartisans. Interestingly, however, both Republican and Democratic women note distinct differences between male and female Members in the way in which they understand problems and work to find a solution. By and large, all of the female Members emphasize that they are more interested in policy development than partisanship and see themselves as consensus-builders.

This chapter illustrates, nonetheless, that partisanship is critical to understanding the position as well as the participation of women within the legislative arena. Women understand themselves as part of the party appa-ratus. To some extent, positions within the institution are granted or taken away based on party support. For Democratic women, this dynamic is not problematic. Their electoral pressures fall in line with the partisan pressures they face within the institution. Republican women, on the other hand, face unique cross-pressures from their district and their party organization. Though we might expect them to pay less attention to party-building activi-ties than Republican men due to their electoral constraints and lower aver-age party support scores, Republican women actually participate equally in all three activities examined in this study. In fact, in the Republican Party, women attend more organizational meetings on average than men; more women have leadership PACs than men; and more women participate in media than men. It seems that women try to compensate for their lack of party-line voting by participating in party-building activities. Yet, women have not seen their efforts pay off in terms of greater representation at the highest levels of leadership.

Female Members have clear sentiments about their participation. Some of these sentiments involve their participation within the party organiza-tion, including: their evaluation of the party leadership and culture, their respective role within the organization, and their behavior relative to their male colleagues. This facet of women's political participation cannot be discovered or understood outside of an examination of partisanship. While this study is by no means comprehensive, it is a first step in understanding the ways in which women's participation is contoured by their involvement in the party organization.

The present analysis holds several implications for women's political participation. First, party culture does influence the ways in which women participate. The Republican Party, with its emphasis on homogeneity, loyalty, elitism, and centralization, is not likely to incorporate women from marginal districts or with liberal ideological leanings into full positions of leadership. Examining the 103rd through 105th Congresses, Ansolabehere, Snyder, and Stewart (2001) suggest that party members may be especially loyal (on procedural) votes because:

> They understand that to be disloyal on such votes risks long-range trouble within the party. The *pattern* of votes cast by a representative is likely to be the critical factor that party leaders use when they judge the rank-and-file, just as voters use patterns of votes to judge their representatives. (Fenno 1978, 151, 559)

The result of this pressure is that moderate members are conflicted. They must either sacrifice constituent responsiveness or career aspirations. Ansolabehere et al. (2001) summarize:

> Our results reveal a fundamental tension between party politics and electoral responsiveness. Parties consistently pull the moderate legislators away from the middle, away from the median voter in the nation as a whole . . . Parties provide greater collective responsibility, but at the cost of policies that deviate from the preference of the median voter. (560)

These findings yield critical implications for the representation of women and the fate of women's issue legislation. Prior to the Republican takeover, Swers (1998) found that Republican women were situated to have the most influence over women's issue legislation. She states:

> Gender plays a most significant role in the voting of Republican representatives. While many women's issues are supported by all Democrats, Republican women are defecting from their party's traditional position to vote in favor of these issues. (445)

She warns, however, that the shift in partisan control of the House might influence this trend, stating:

> Given the pivotal role of these legislators, the Republican takeover of Congress in 1994 makes the position of Republican women even more significant in

determining outcomes on women's issue voting. Yet the newly elected Republican women of the 104th Congress were ideologically more conservative than were the Republican congresswomen of the 103rd Congress. (444)

It should be noted that Republican women were positioned in leadership roles during the politics surrounding the Republican Revolution and the Republican Convention of 1996. As women's numbers have grown in the party in recent years, however, their numbers in leadership have decreased. We are left to wonder if the early success of women was due to tokenism rather than full incorporation within the Republican Party. Of particular concern should be women's satisfaction with the party in light of the Republican Party's tendency to bypass seniority and reward party loyalty when allocating leadership positions. "The motivation to remain in Congress is diminished when members feel isolated from their party, from large portions of their voting constituents, and from the opportunity to occupy positions of influence within the Congress" (Moore and Hibbing 1998, 1105).

The Democratic Party, on the other hand, with its emphasis on diversity, dialogue, equality, and decentralization, would seem to be more likely to incorporate women into positions of leadership within the committee and party structures. After all, these women represent some of the most Democratic districts in the country. Nonetheless, women's ascension within the party organization has been quite gradual and limited to positions of supportive rather than full leadership. While women are perhaps more likely to be given leadership positions within the Democratic Party, these positions are also more likely to involve their gender. For example, a few female Democratic Members did mention leadership roles, but these leadership roles involved liaisoning with leadership from the Women's Caucus. Republican women might not be as readily incorporated into leadership, but their inclusion (as more than just tokens) would be based on criteria other than their gender.

Chapter 5

The Matrix of Women's Participation in Congress

Introduction

We began this journey with a few simple questions: Do Republican women behave the same way as Democratic women? Do they vote alike? Are their priorities the same? Do they have the same level of success within the institution? In other words, does gender alone determine legislative behavior, or does partisanship also influence the way in which women participate? To address these questions we examined the participation of female Members in the congressional district, on the floor of the U.S. House of Representatives, and in the party organization. In all of these arenas we found clear answers. It is certain from this analysis that just as Swers (2002, 15) notes, "Policy is not made in a vacuum. Members are highly affected by the demands of their party caucus and leaders as well as the external political climate around them" (Rhode 1991; Cox and McCubbins 1993; Sinclair 1995). Whether a female Member is a Democrat or a Republican, partisanship is an important factor of the political context serving to shape women's political experience. Female Republican Members do not behave the same way as female Democratic Members. They do not vote the same way on the floor. They do not have the same priorities. And, in the end, while it appears they have some level of success within the Congress, the factors predicting this success are unique to the parties to which they belong.

Partisanship is not the only important factor in the political context. Other factors such as Member goal motivations are also involved in determining behavior. In other words, whether a Member is concerned with reelection, policy, or prestige serves to shape participation within the Congress. We found women focused on their reelection, as indicated by the staff for the Republican Member who stated:

> She (Republican female Member) couldn't ever run for leadership because she's too busy securing her own race. But she would have been great (in leadership) because none of them are from vulnerable districts. She anticipates the train or the storm and would be a good spot check. If something is going to happen, she's the first to hear the rumbling.

We found women focused on their policy priorities, such as the Democratic Member who stated, "As a physician, they (leadership) think I'm kind of an expert (on health issues) . . . . They see me as a leader in healthcare . . . as someone they can depend on."

In some instances, women clearly indicated the role social identity played in influencing their policy priorities. As one female Democratic Member suggested:

> Some of them (male Members) aren't as sensitive to issues important to minorities as I would like for them to be . . . seeing how that connects to the nation's healthcare as a whole. They get tired of me talking about the same issue, and don't see it as important.

Finally, we found women focused on their own prestige within the institution, such as Minority Leader Nancy Pelosi (D-CA) who reached a level of institutional leadership unprecedented in American history.

In the end, however, it appears that all goals, whether they are reelection, policy, power, or prestige related, are not pursued in a vacuum. Partisanship matters. The two major political parties are distinguished by unique cultures that permeate the electoral, institutional, and organizational elements of our political system. Female Members, like male Members, participate within the parameters of these two political parties and reflect their distinctive cultures.

Secondly, Member behavior is predictive given that it is motivated by distinct, identifiable goals. Pursuit of Member goals is structured by the party cultures. Women must conform to their partisan cultures in order to achieve their respective goals. In order to understand the implications of women's behavior within our Congress, we must account for the parameters created by partisanship and Member goals including reelection. In the end, these party cultures determine the "playing field" on which women succeed or fail.

Theoretical Contribution

The two parties demonstrate distinct patterns of behavior. Republican party culture is defined by ideological homogeneity, party loyalty, internal competition, hierarchical organization, and elite participation. Democratic party culture, on the other hand, is defined by ideological as well as descriptive diversity, constituent responsiveness, seniority rule, and egalitarian organization and participation (see Freeman 1986).

Partisanship structures the electoral circumstance of women, and thus influences their voting behavior, allocation of resources, prioritization of goals, and participation in partisan activities. Partisanship is further associated with male Members' attitudes toward and evaluations of their female co-partisans within the institution. Interestingly, while Democratic male and female Members articulate gender differences, these differences are not apparent in voting behavior. Contrastingly, while Republican male and female Members do not articulate gender differences, there are significant gendered differences in the voting behavior of Republican female Members. Women do define themselves as partisans and do operate within the context and confines of their party organizations.

Not only do Members consider themselves as partisans, they are also driven by a number of identifiable goals, including reelection, policy, and prestige (Fenno 1973; Mayhew 1974). Parker (1992) suggests that Members try to expand their electoral security to attain the discretion necessary to pursue their institutional goals. In order to understand women's participation it is imperative to consider these goals as influencing their legislative choices.

In sum, we find a matrix within which Members of Congress must operate. Partisanship structures the attainment of Member goals, including the basic goal of reelection. And reciprocally, goal motivations can impinge upon participation in the party organization, thus limiting institutional effectiveness. As presented in the first chapter, table 1.3 illustrates how party culture combines with electoral security to create a matrix of Member behavior.

For Democratic Members electoral security provides them the freedom to pursue personal goals whether they involve power, policy, or prestige. Electoral security is usually associated with seniority. In other words, the longer a Member holds a congressional seat, the greater the Member's incumbency advantage over any potential challenger and the greater the electoral margin by which the Member wins elections. This seniority not only provides Democratic Members with electoral security but also with institutional status and partisan leadership positions. Democrats strictly follow the seniority rule for allocating positions of power.

Marginal Democratic Members, on the other hand, lack electoral discretion, and thus must focus their attention on district concerns. It is important to recognize that their partisan culture allows them the discretion to vote and participate in the interest of their districts. They are limited, however, within the institution because of their lack of seniority, but with time they can expect all the advantages that seniority brings.

Republican Members, contrastingly, face altogether different circumstances within this framework. Electorally safe Republicans enjoy the freedom to pursue their personal goals, but they must pursue them within the parameters of the party platform in order to be effective within the organization. Seniority plays a small role outside of these party parameters. Even the most senior Members can expect to be overlooked for leadership positions if they do not conform their pursuits to the party platform.

Electorally vulnerable Republican Members also operate within this system of ideological and participatory homogeneity, but lack the freedom to ignore district interests. In order to secure their reelection, they at times must stray from the partisan fold. Not only do they not adhere to the party platform, they also lack the personal or partisan resources to compete for leadership positions.

From this analysis, we develop a much richer understanding of Member behavior than that offered by previous studies. We understand Members as operating in a complex, dynamic legislative arena, both structuring and structured by their participation in it. We see party organizations truly as mediating institutions that not only impact Members' voting behavior, but also impact their behavior both inside and outside of Congress. Furthermore, we appreciate parties as the professional and central organizations that they are, inherently structuring Members' goals of power, policy, and prestige. Specifically, we develop a critical understanding of the role of parties and partisanship in structuring women's political participation within the Congress. The two party cultures serve to both advance and limit women's access to political power in the contemporary context.

Methodological Contribution

One of the most important contributions of this study is its combination of quantitative and qualitative data. The quantitative data for this book spans a full decade and five congresses (103rd to 107th Congresses). It integrates district-level census data and electoral vote returns with Member-level data in order to control for situational factors in predicting ideological voting behavior. The qualitative data incorporates interview data with party organizational records to more fully capture the complex partisan environment in which Members operate. The interview data includes twenty-five Member interviews, forty-seven congressional staff interviews, and nine party elite interviews—a total of eighty-one interviews. For a more thorough presentation of the interview data, refer to the Appendix.

Second, this analysis recognizes the significance of multiple measures of participation (Hall 1996). Analysis of Member partisan participation at both the institutional and organizational level more fully captures the relationship of party culture and legislative behavior. By examining women's legislative behavior at the electoral, institutional, and organizational level, we develop a more holistic understanding of female Members' political circumstance. Future studies of congressional behavior should attempt to bring together the disparate worlds in which Members operate. As Fenno (1990) states:

> My own view begins with the idea that politicians are both goal-seeking and situation-interpreting individuals. It proceeds to the idea that politicians act on the basis of what they want to accomplish in their world, and on the basis of how they interpret what they see in that world. It moves from there to the idea that we can gain valuable knowledge of their actions, perceptions, and interpretations by trying to see their world as they see it. (114)

Findings

Political parties structure the legislative behavior of female Members of Congress. Female legislators participate within the context of their respective party culture. From this simple argument, we embarked upon a rich study of women's legislative behavior within the context of partisanship. This journey revealed important differences in female Members' behavior at multiple levels of participation: in the electoral arena, in the institution of the U.S. House of Representatives, and in the party organization.

Participation in the Electorate

Within the electorate, female congressional candidates' partisanship structures their political circumstance in distinct and significant ways. Female Republican candidates come from particular backgrounds, typically including political families or previous legislative or business experience. Republican women typically represent moderate districts that are fiscally conservative but socially more liberal than the party mean. One reason for this is that they may suffer from gendered stereotypes that inhibit their ability to succeed in more conservative districts (McDermott 1997). Female politicians are often viewed as being liberal on social issues regardless of their record or personal platform simply based on their gender identity (Plutzer and Zipp 1996; McDermott 1997). For this reason, female Republican candidates often face difficult primary elections against more conservative challengers, and difficult general elections against more liberal opponents. Consequently, they must devote substantial resources to constituent service and electoral concerns throughout the legislative cycle.

On average, Republican women represent more marginal districts than any other Members of Congress. Not only are their districts more ideologically liberal than the districts represented by Republican men, their electoral wins are also more marginal than that of their male colleagues. Not only do female Republican Members see their districts as requiring more attention because of ideological disparities, they also understand their personal ambition constrained by electoral demands.

Democratic women, on the other hand, face altogether different circumstances. They run on social issues and come from backgrounds in social work, local government, and civil service. They typically represent very liberal districts that value diversity and expect liberal voting records. Often winning by large margins, they have more time and resources to spend on other things besides electoral concerns.

Participation in the Institution

Partisanship combines with electoral needs to structure women's political circumstance within the institution of the U.S. Congress as well. Female Republican Members embark upon their legislative careers with little electoral security. They face the constant threat of a tough primary as well as general race. They lack the time, resources, or legislative discretion to pursue goals within the institution. Their male Republican colleagues, while appreciating the women's role in maintaining swing districts, expect the women nonetheless to vote in lockstep, and hold the women's moderate voting records against them when electing or appointing partisan officers.

Democratic women, on the other hand, often enter their legislative career with wide electoral margins. They enjoy the bloc vote of minority populations and rarely face difficult electoral competition. This circumstance provides them with ample time, resources, and legislative discretion to pursue their personal goals whether they involve policy development or career advancement. Male Democratic Members value the diversity provided by female Members, appreciate their outspokenness on social issues, and expect them to reflect the interests and concerns of their districts. These women operate within a partisan system that rewards seniority regardless of ideological orientation, voting record, or partisan activity.

Differences between Republican party culture and Democratic party culture within the institution is further illustrated by the explanatory power of the models predicting ideological voting behavior. The model predicting ideological voting behavior performed differently for Democrats and Republicans. The only common significant predictor between the two parties was the general ideology of the district. In terms of strength, significance, and direction, all of the other indicators in the model performed differently for the two parties. This suggests that the constituency constraints faced by Members vary by party, and the responsiveness of Members to these pressures also varies by party.

Further, when controlling for district- and Member-level variables, the model predicts nearly half the variance in Democratic voting behavior across congresses. Contrastingly, the model generally predicts less than a quarter of the variance in Republican voting behavior across congresses. This observation illuminates one of the primary cultural differences between these two parties. The Republican Party encourages ideological homogeneity and does not encourage or reward constituent services. Contrastingly, the Democratic Party encourages diversity, coalition-building, and equal representation. One way in which to conceptualize these different party cultures is to understand the Republican Party as conforming more to a responsible-party model of representation and the Democratic Party as conforming more to a constituency-centered model of representation.

Participation in the Party Organization

Finally, within the party organizations themselves, female Member's participation is structured by their respective party cultures. Republican women must join Republican men in competing for positions of party leadership. In these races, they must articulate and emphasize credentials other than their gender when bidding for their colleagues' vote or the approval of the Steering Committee. They must further rely on a solid voting record demonstrating strong Republicanism. They must participate in party-building activities, such as generating party money through fundraising and communicating the party message through the media.

On the other hand, Democratic women operate within a party culture that values seniority over competition and diversity over ideology. Democratic women are valued as political pioneers. They have a place at the leadership table simply because of the demographic they represent. While at the highest levels of leadership they must be competitive in order to win, once senior, they are generally granted full access to positions of leadership within the institution and organization.

While women of both parties have enjoyed access to positions both in the extended leadership structure and in the committee structure, they have not had much enduring success in securing positions at the highest levels of these structures. Until very recently, women had only sporadically held full committee chairmanships and had never been part of the formal leadership team. During the first session of the 107th Congress, however, the Democratic Caucus elected Rep. Nancy Pelosi (D-CA) to the position of Minority Whip. This represents the highest congressional office ever held by a woman. During the 108th Congress, the Democratic Caucus further elected Pelosi to the position of Minority Leader, and the Republican Conference elected Deborah Pryce (R-OH) to the position of Conference Chair.

Based on the different cultures of the Democratic and Republican Parties, it is not surprising that a Democratic woman would make this historical achievement. The implications of this book, nonetheless, suggest that there are multiple forces at work to limit the effectiveness of women within the Republican Party besides general party ethos. Republican women, unlike Democratic women, face electoral constraints that limit their organizational ambition. Another consequence of their electoral circumstance is that Republican women lack the legislative discretion to vote with the party and thus do not prove themselves ideologically loyal enough to hold positions of power.

It does appear that Republican women are disadvantaged within the party organization. Using multiple measures of partisan support, Republican women participate equally with their male colleagues in party-building activities. Perhaps their participation is an attempt to compensate for their divergent voting behavior. Nonetheless, female Republican Members enjoy only limited positional status within the party. The voting discretion they need to ensure their reelection has consequences for them within the hierarchy of the party organization. It is important to realize that:

> Voters, constituents, groups, and party leaders are the ultimate principals in the legislative process, and members of Congress are their agents. A major problem inherent in, and disruptive of, the principal-agent relationship is the exercise of discretion: discretion occurs when agents pursue their own interests while ignoring the preferences of their principals. A natural remedy for this problem is to invest resources into monitoring the agent's actions, especially since issues such as moral hazard create a divergence between the principal's interest and agent's actions. It is costly, however, for principals to monitor the

actions of their agents since the full observation of actions is either impossible or prohibitively costly. (Parker 1992, 10–11)

The costs of monitoring Republican women's legislative behavior outweigh the benefits of their descriptive representation among leadership. Given this dynamic, it is surprising that Republican women have had as much success as they have had in securing other positions including: seats on exclusive committees, subcommittee chairmanships, and seats on partisan committees and leadership teams.

Two Models of Member Participation

From these findings, we develop two distinct systems of Member participation. For Democrats, the system is what we would consider traditional. Figure 5.1 illustrates the typical path of participation of Democratic Members of Congress. Although the cultural characteristics of the party, the characteristics of the district, and the characteristics of the Member all interact during the election, they ultimately result in a vote return for the

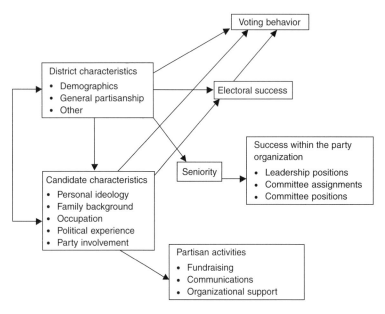

Figure 5.1   Model of the Democratic system

Member that communicates his or her electoral safety in the district. This factor along with district and Member preferences lead to the Member's general voting behavior. In terms of partisan activities, however, voting is not a prominent criterion. The Member's personal political background might influence his or her involvement in partisan activities. The Member's electoral security might also figure into his or her decision to allocate resources in party-building activities. In the end, however, the seniority of the Member is a large determinant of the Member's supportive activities in the party organization. Seniority in turn is also largely associated with success within the organization. Party leaders are senior Members, regardless of their voting behavior.

Figure 5.2 illustrates the Republican system of participation. Just as in the Democratic model, party culture, district, and candidate characteristics all interact to produce election outcomes. In turn, these electoral outcomes shape Member voting behavior and partisan activity. What is noticeably different in the Republican system is the lack of seniority as a determinant of both partisan activity and success within the party organization. Candidate characteristics are important to partisan activity. Members who were involved with their state and local party organizations are likely to participate in party-building activities in the national organization. Members who are electorally safe are also more likely to invest resources in party-building activities than electorally marginal Members. In the competitive climate of Republican party culture, these activities lead to success within the organization. Similarly, given the value of ideological homogeneity in the Republican party culture, voting behavior also is associated with success in the organization. These two factors figure much more prominently than seniority in the Republican organizational system.

Implications for Women in Politics

The present analysis holds several theoretical implications for the future study of women's legislative behavior as well as practical implications for women's participation in the legislative arena. That the models predicting Member voting behavior performed differently for the two parties bears significant implications for future models of representation. Not only does the party culture of the Democratic Party provide more legislative discretion to its Members to respond to electoral pressures, Democratic Members in turn respond more to district voting cues than Republican Members. Future models of voting behavior should take into account differences in party culture and the ensuing differences in the strength and significance of

133

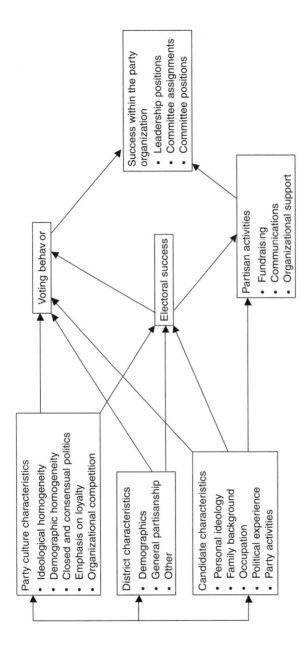

Figure 5.2 Model of the Republican system

indicators of ideological voting. From this analysis, it appears that the Democratic Party adheres to a more constituency-centered model of representation while the Republican Party reflects a more responsible-party model of representation. Perhaps Miller and Stokes (1963) were right in asserting:

> No single tradition of representation fully accords with the realities of American legislative politics. The American system *is* a mixture, to which the Burkean, instructed-delegate, and responsible-party models all can be said to have contributed elements. (56)

The Republican Party, in contrast to the culture of the Democratic Party, does not value diversity and coalition-building. Republican Members do not respond to constituency pressures to the same extent as Democratic Members. This poses particular problems for female Republican Members who represent the most liberal Republican districts. Republican women face unique electoral pressures that must shape their legislative behavior. Because they operate within a party culture that values homogeneity and party loyalty, however, their divergent voting behavior poorly positions them within the party organization.

The second implication of this analysis more broadly involves future work in congressional behavior. The argument of this book crosses prominent theoretical frameworks such as gender theory, party culture theory, and rational choice theory to provide a more comprehensive and more accurate theory of women's legislative behavior. Concepts such as discretion and the reelection incentive hold important ramifications for women's legislative behavior that current gender theory overlooks. Future theoretical work should not be constrained to one framework or set of frameworks, but should aim to accurately reflect the political world by bringing to bear relevant theory.

While gender theory has largely neglected the unique role of Republican women in the Congress, it is precisely these women who are demonstrating noticeably gendered voting behavior. This analysis builds on the work of Swers (1998), who suggests, "much of the impact of gender is due to the influence of Republican women" (1998, 435; 2002). Given the district and institutional circumstance of Democratic women in Congress, there are no significant differences between their behavior and that of their male colleagues. Their voting records are generally identical with those of Democratic men. This analysis does not explore the substance of women's legislative activities, and thus perhaps overlooks the impact Democratic women have in both developing and championing "women's issue" legislation. Nonetheless, in terms of general ideological voting behavior, Democratic women do not demonstrate unique behavior.

The gendered voting behavior demonstrated by Republican women leads us to some significant implications. It is important to recognize that, in light of their political circumstance, Republican women are choosing to pursue policy success over partisan success and are thus stifling their congressional careers. This observation raises critical questions concerning women's political behavior. Do these Republican women know that they are limiting their potential for success within the party organization by voting with a gender consciousness? Could it be that these women have so very few role models to emulate, and have until recently been unaware of any repercussions of gendered behavior, that they are making the same mistakes as those who have gone before them? Now that Marge Roukema (R-NJ), the most senior Member to vie for the chairmanship position on the Banking Committee during the organization of the 107th Congress, was denied a chairmanship at the end of her career, will other Republican women take note and begin to pattern themselves even more like their male Republican colleagues in order to be effective? Or will they still choose to pursue policy that targets women's issues?

In the end, there also are several practical implications of this analysis. First, the finding that women operate within two separate party organizations with distinct cultures leads to several implications concerning women's participation within the institution of the U.S. House of Representatives. Democratic women enjoy a partisan climate that fosters ideological diversity and equitable participation. The organizational structure is reflected best by spokes on a wheel, with the different coalitions such as the Congressional Black Caucus, the Women's Caucus, the Progressive Caucus, the New Democrats, and the Blue Dogs all equally represented. Democratic women, for the most part, represent districts ideologically compatible with the party's liberal stance on issues. Republican women, on the other hand, operate within a partisan climate that fosters ideological homogeneity and organizational competition. The organizational structure is reflected best by a hierarchical structure, with no specific representation of coalitions such as the Tuesday Group or the Value Action Team.

How do these partisan climates impact on the participation of women within the institution? For Democratic women, this organizational dynamic fosters their equitable participation. Although we might expect these women to be advantaged because of the party's promotion of descriptive diversity, it is also important to remember the premium Democrats place on seniority. While women will ultimately enjoy full access to positions of leadership within the Democratic Party, they must gain the seniority necessary to be granted these positions. Republican women face a very different organizational dynamic. The Republican Party traditionally has not valued ideological diversity, but rather has emphasized and rewarded ideological homogeneity. Republicans also place little value on descriptive diversity or seniority. Rather, the party seems to reward organizational and ideological support. While women are not limited by their lack of seniority, they are limited by their electoral circumstances and ideological preferences.

Take, for example, the leadership bid of Rep. Jennifer Dunn (R-WA). In the leadership elections for the 106th Congress in 1998 she ran for the position of House Majority Leader along with Rep. Steve Largent (R-OK) against the sitting Majority Leader, Richard Armey (R-TX). With Republicans questioning her stance on moral issues such as abortion in the years following the Contract with America, Dunn had begun to vote more conservatively on these issues and had been elected Conference Vice Chair in 1996 for the 105th Congress. "Despite her leadership credentials and her efforts to allay the fears of social conservatives, Dunn was eliminated in the early rounds of balloting" (Swers 2002, 279). Even after losing the race for Majority Leader, Dunn worked with Largent to offer the Republican response to President Bill Clinton's State of the Union Address in 1999.

Unlike Marge Roukema (R-NJ), who carried a moderate voting record and was denied a committee leadership position, the treatment of Dunn suggests that the implications of Republican party culture for female Members are very serious and threaten to limit even rather conservative women's leadership aspirations. Swers suggests:

> Dunn's inability to gain the support of conservative party members concerned about her abortion record contributed to her defeat and cost her access to the rewards of party leadership. After Armey announced his plans to retire in 2002, Dunn responded to questions about her future leadership ambitions by stating that "I've always said there should be a woman in the top leadership. Someone with a different set of experiences. . . . We'll see what develops." (ibid., 279–280)

The implications of this analysis, however, stretch beyond the current participation of women in Congress. According to Bernick (2001), "legislative career orientation (is) associated with attainment of a leadership position, political ambition, and acceptance of legislative norms" (123). If women are not effective as participants, they will become disenchanted with the institution and choose to focus their efforts elsewhere. Recent works suggests that institutional ineffectiveness is directly correlated with Member retirement (Theriault 1998). As Moore and Hibbing (1998) state: "members who are not achieving their goals are more likely than others to depart voluntarily from the U.S. House" (1088).

This is perhaps most disturbing given the current partisan control of the House of Representatives. At the time of this analysis, Republicans hold the majority in the House, thus female Republican Members enjoy the most political opportunity to influence the workings of the Congress. Nonetheless, Republican women lack the time, resources, or partisan influence necessary to effect change. They lack the electoral discretion to be effective participants within the party organization. Based on this scenario, we might expect Republican women to become disenchanted with the institution and seek early retirement.

Conversely, we should expect Democratic women to enjoy full participation within the party structure. They not only enjoy the legislative discretion to develop policy and influence the party as a group, they also enjoy the electoral discretion to fully participate within the party organization. Based on this alternative scenario, we should expect Democratic women to remain in Congress. It is important to recognize, however, that another factor leading to early retirement is persistent minority status with the institution (Gilmour and Rothstein 1993). If Democrats do not regain the majority, we might expect Democratic women to become frustrated by their inability to effect change given their minority partisan status, and seek early retirement as well.

At present, the political climate for women is intensely structured by partisanship. Women's fate within the institution largely depends on the status and cultures of the two major parties. These cultures permeate the electoral, institutional, and organizational aspects of the American Congress. In the electorate, party culture structures every aspect of campaigns and elections, determining both who runs and who wins. In the institution, party culture structures the committee system and the policy agenda, determining who has power and how they exercise it. Finally, party culture structures the party organizations in Congress, resulting in distinct leadership structures, roads to power, and modes of participation.

It is insufficient to only understand women's increased inclusion in the Congress as leading to a more liberal voice on legislation, particularly on issues directly affecting women and children. It is insufficient to simply understand women's increased inclusion as leading to an alternative political dynamic, increasing collaborative behavior among legislators and female leadership. Whether a woman is a Democrat or a Republican matters. It defines the political context in which women can pursue their goals and influence the debate. We must understand the specific ways in which partisanship structures women's participation in order to begin truly to comprehend how women are making a difference within the American Congress.

Appendix

Both quantitative and qualitative data were used in this book to explore the electoral circumstances of women in Congress given their partisanship. The quantitative data included descriptive Member indicators, such as the Member's biological sex and party affiliation, as well as district indicators, such as the vote return for the Member and the presidential vote return of the district in the last election. The sex of the Member was coded 1 for female and 0 for male. The party affiliation of the Member was coded 1 for Republican and 0 for Democrat. Independents were excluded from the analysis. Both of these descriptive indicators were taken from *The National Journal's Almanac of American Politics* (1994–2002). District indicators were also taken from this source and were coded as the percent of the vote received multiplied by 100 for ease of interpretation. For presentation of variables and coding, refer to table A1.

Table A1 Variable descriptions and coding

Dependent variables	
DW-NOMINATE scores	Range between −1 and +1 on one liberal–conservative dimension, with −1 being the most liberal and +1 being the most conservative.
Social liberalism ratings	Range between 0 and 100 on one liberal–conservative dimension, with 0 being the most conservative and 100 being the most liberal.
Party unity scores	Range between 0 and 100 on one dimension, with 0 being never unified with the party vote and 100 being completely unified with the party vote.
Independent variables	
Female	Dichotomous variable accounting for Members' biological sex; coded 0 = male; 1 = female.
Seniority	Variable accounting for Members' seniority; coded as years in office.
Electoral marginality	Dichotomous variable accounting for Members' electoral insecurity; coded 0 = safe, or receiving atleast 60% of the district vote in the last election; 1 = marginal, or receiving less than 60% of the district vote in the last election.

Table A1 Continued

Female electoral marginality	Interaction term combining Member sex with Member electoral marginality; coded dichotomously with 0 = safe male, safe female, or marginal male; 1 = marginal female.
% Black	Variable measuring the percentage of the district population that is African American; taken from the 1990 Census.
Socioeconomic character of the district	Factor score measuring the socioeconomic makeup of the district. Data reduction of the % rural, the % college-educated, and the average per capita income of the district.
Presidential vote return of the district	Variable measuring the percent of the district vote taken by the winning presidential candidate in 1992, 1996, or 2000.
Leadership PAC	Variable measuring affiliation with a leadership PAC; coded dichotomously as 0 = no affiliation; 1 = affiliation.
Media participation	Variable measuring participation in media; coded dichotomously as 0 = participation; 1 = no participation.
Leadership team	Variable measuring position on leadership team; coded dichotomously as 0 = position; 1 = no position.
Party-building activities	Factor score measuring the party-building activities of the Member. Data reduction of affiliation with a leadership PAC, participation in media, and member of leadership team.

The qualitative data for this book came from personal interviews with staff and Members in Washington, D.C. between June and December of the first session of the 107th Congress (2001). Along with congressional staff, the respondents also include staff of the political and organizational arms of the national parties, including: the National Republican Campaign Committee, the House Republican Conference, the Democratic Caucus, and the National Federation of Republican Women. All together, forty-seven staff interviews, twenty-five Member interviews, and nine party elite interviews comprise the bulk of the qualitative data for the book. Table A2 provides a classification scheme based on party and sex.

The interviews were semi-structured, involving a series of open-ended questions concerning legislative priorities, group membership, campaigning, evaluations of the party organizations and personal roles, and perceived gender and partisan differences among colleagues. Specific questions of Members of

Table A2   Classification of interviews

Affiliation	Total
Republican Member	**17**
Female	10
Male	7
Republican Party Elite	**8**
Republican Congressional Aide	**29**
For Female Member	13
For Male Member	16
Democratic Member	**8**
Female	6
Male	2
Democratic Party Elite	**1**
Democratic Congressional Aide	**18**
For Female Member	7
For Male Member	11
Total	81

Congress included:

- What do you consider to be your top three legislative priorities?
- What legislation do you consider to be landmark since you've been in Congress?
- Of what informal groups or organizations do you consider yourself an active member?
- What do you most identify with the Democratic/Republican Party?
- What do you value most about the party?
- What do you see as your own personal role in the party organization?
- If you could have any Member of Congress run your next campaign, who would it be and why?
- How do you see yourself as similar to or different from your female Democratic/Republican (of opposite party) colleagues?
- How do you see yourself as similar to or different from your male Democratic/Republican (of same party) colleagues?

This data was supplemented with interviews of congressional staff and party elite. The questions asked of these respondents were more for background information than anything else. Some of these questions included:

- What interested the Member in running for political office?
- Was the Member recruited by the party, or voluntarily ran for office?
- What kinds of party organizational meetings are you aware of that the Member is regularly invited to?

- How regularly does the Member attend these meetings?
- Approximately how often does the Member attend party fund-raisers?
- Does the Member do fund-raisers in other districts for colleagues?
- What do you think the Member values the most about party membership?

These questions helped to verify both findings from the quantitative data used to measure Member party-building activities as well as qualitative data gathered from interviews with Members themselves.

During the data collection for this analysis, the nation underwent a serious terrorist attack on September 11, 2001, that dramatically shifted the policy agenda and partisan mood. Fortunately, most of the interviews had already been conducted. There were, however, notable differences in the responses during the weeks immediately following September 11, 2001. During this period of bipartisanship, Members of both parties were less likely to discuss differences between them and their colleagues across the aisle. Due to the semi-structured nature of the interviews, most of the interview data mirror that gathered before this critical event. Certain direct references to the event are excluded from the analysis to provide a more consistent picture of Member behavior.

Bibliography

Aistrup, Joseph. 1996. *The Southern Strategy Revisted*. Lexington: The University of Kentucky Press.

Aldrich, John H. and David W. Rohde. 2000. The Republican Revolution and the House Appropriations Committee. *The Journal of Politics* 62(1): 1–33.

———. 1997. The Transition to Republican Rule in the House: Implications for Theories of Congressional Politics. *Political Science Quarterly* 112(4): 541–567.

Almond, Gabriel A. and Sidney Verba. 1965. *Civic Culture*. Boston: Little, Brown.

Andres, Gary J. 1999. Observations on a Post-Gingrich House. *PS: Political Science and Politics* 32(3): 571–574.

Ansolabehere, Stephen, James M. Snyder, Jr., and Charles Stewart, III. 2001. The Effects of Party and Preferences on Congressional Roll-Call Voting. *Legislative Studies Quarterly* 26(4): 533–572.

Baer, Denise. 1993. Political Parties: the Missing Variable in Women and Politics Research. *Political Research Quarterly* 46(1): 547–576.

Bales, Robert F. 1950. *Interaction Process Analysis: A Method for the Study of Small Groups*. Cambridge, MA: Addison-Wesley.

Barone, Michael and Grant Ujifusa. 1993. *The Almanac of American Politics 1994*. Washington, D.C.: National Journal.

———. 1995. *The Almanac of American Politics 1996*. Washington, D.C.: National Journal.

———. 1997. *The Almanac of American Politics 1998*. Washington, D.C.: National Journal.

———. 1999. *The Almanac of American Politics 2000*. Washington, D.C.: National Journal.

———. 2001. *The Almanac of American Politics 2002*. Washington, D.C.: National Journal.

Berelson, Bernard, Paul Lazarsfeld, and William McPhee. 1954. *Voting*. Chicago: University of Chicago Press.

Bernick, F. Lee. 2001. Anchoring Legislative Careers. *Legislative Studies Quarterly* 26: 123–143.

Bianco, William T. 1984. Strategic Decisions on Candidacy in U.S. Congressional Districts. *Legislative Studies Quarterly* 2: 351–364.

Biersack, Robert and Paul S. Herrnson. 1994. Political Parties and the Year of the Woman. In *The Year of the Woman: Myths and Realities*, eds. Elizabeth Adell Cook, Sue Thomas, and Clyde Wilcox. Boulder, CO: Westview Press.

Bledsoe, Timothy and Mary Herring. 1990. Victims of Circumstance: Women in Pursuit of Political Office. *The American Political Science Review* 84(1): 213–223.

Bond, Jon R. 1983. The Influence of Constituency Diversity on Electoral Competition in Voting for Congress, 1974–1978. *Legislative Studies Quarterly* 8: 201–217.

Bond, Jon R., Kristin Campbell, and James B. Cottrill. 2001. The Puzzle of Constituency Diversity Revisited: Conditional Effects of District Diversity on Competition in Congressional Elections. Presented at the Southern Political Science Associational Meeting. Atlanta, GA (November 7–10, 2001).

Bond, Jon R., Gary Covington, and Richard Fleisher. 1985. Explaining Challenger Quality in Congressional Elections. *The Journal of Politics* 47: 510–529.

Brady, David W. 1972. Congressional Leadership and Party Voting in the McKinley Era: A Comparison to the Modern House. *Midwest Journal of Political Science* 16(3): 439–459.

———. 1973. A Research Note on the Impact of Interparty Competition on Congressional Voting in a Competitive Era. *The American Political Science Review* 67(1): 153–156.

Brandes Crook, Sara and John R. Hibbing. 1985. Congressional Reform and Party Discipline: The Effects of Changes in the Seniority System on Party Loyalty in the US House of Representatives. *British Journal of Political Science* 15(2): 207–226.

Brewer, Mark D., Mack D. Mariani, and Jeffrey M. Stonecash. 2002. Northern Democrats and Party Polarization in the U.S. House. *Legislative Studies Quarterly* 27(3): 423–444.

Brunell, T. L., W. Koetzel, J. Dinardo, B. Grofman, and S. L. Feld. 1999. The $R^2 = .93$: Where Then Do They Differ? Comparing Liberal and Conservative Interest Group Ratings. *Legislative Studies Quarterly* 24(1): 87–101.

Bullock, Charles S., III. 1973. Committee Transfers in the United States House of Representatives. *The Journal of Politics* 35(1): 85–120.

Bullock, Charles S., III and Patricia Lee Findley Hays. 1972. Recruitment of Women for Congress. *Western Political Quarterly* 25: 416–423.

Burrell, Barbara. 1994. *A Woman's Place Is in the House: Campaigning for Congress in the Feminist Era*. Ann Arbor: University of Michigan Press.

———. 1998. Campaign Finance: Women's Experience in the Modern Era. In *Women and Elective Office*, eds. Sue Thomas and Clyde Wilcox. New York: Oxford University Press.

Campbell, A., P. E. Converse, W. E. Miller, and D. E. Stokes. 1960. *The American Voter*. Chicago: University of Chicago Press.

Canon, David T. 1990. *Actors, Athletes, and Astronauts: Political Amateurs in the United States Congress*. Chicago, IL: University of Chicago Press.

Cantor, D. M. and Paul S. Herrnson. 1997. Party Campaign Activity and Party Unity in the U.S. House of Representatives. *Legislative Studies Quarterly* 22(3): 393–415.

Carmines, E. G., J. P. McIver, and J. A. Stimson. 1987. Unrealized Partisanship: A Theory of Dealignment. *The Journal of Politics* 49: 376–400.

Carroll, Susan J. 1985. *Women as Candidates in American Politics*. Bloomington: Indiana University Press.

———. 1994. *Women as Candidates in American Politics*, 2nd ed. Bloomington: Indiana University Press.

———. 2002. Representing Women: Congresswomen's Perceptions of Their Representational Roles. In *Women Transforming Congress*, ed. Cindy S. Rosenthal. Norman, OK: University of Oklahoma Press.

Center for American Women in Politics. 2002. Women in the U.S. House of Representatives: 2002. Accessed from http://www.cawp.rutgers.edu/Facts/Officeholders/house.pdf. Eagleton Institute of Politics, Rutgers, The State University of New Jersey.

Center for Responsive Politics. 2004. Leaders PACs: PAC Contributions to Federal Candidates. Accessed from http://www.opensecrets.org/pacs/industry.asp?txt=Q03&cycle=2004.

Clapp, Charles. 1964. *The Congressman: His Work as He Sees It*. Garden City, NY: Anchor Books.

Clucas, Richard A. 1997. Party Contributions and the Influence of Campaign Committee Chairs on Roll-Call Voting. *Legislative Studies Quarterly* 22(2): 179–194.

Coleman, James S. 1990. *Foundations of Social Theory*. Cambridge, MA: Harvard University Press.

Committee on Political Parties of the American Political Science Association. 1950. Toward a More Responsible Two Party System. *American Political Science Review* 44 (supplement).

Congressional Quarterly Press. *Congressional Quarterly Almanac* 33(1B). Washington, D.C.: Congressional Quarterly Press.

Congressional Quarterly Press. 1993. *Politics in America 1994: The 103rd Congress*. Washington, D.C.: Congressional Quarterly Press.

———. 1995. *Politics in America 1996: The 104th Congress*. Washington, D.C.: Congressional Quarterly Press.

———. 1997. *Politics in America 1998: The 105th Congress*. Washington, D.C.: Congressional Quarterly Press.

———. 1999. *Politics in America 2000: The 106th Congress*. Washington, D.C.: Congressional Quarterly Press.

———. 2001. *Politics in America 2002: The 107th Congress*. Washington, D.C.: Congressional Quarterly Press.

Cooper, Joseph and David Brady. 1981. Institutional Context and Leadership Style: The House from Cannon to Rayburn. *American Political Science Review* 75: 411–425.

Connelly, William F., Jr. and John J. Pitney, Jr. 1999. The House Republicans: Lessons for Political Science. In *New Majority or Old Minority?: The Impact of Republicans on Congress*, eds. Nicol C. Rae and Colton C. Campbell. Lanham, MD: Rowman & Littlefield.

Connelly, William F., Jr. and John J. Pitney, Jr. 1994. The Future of the House Republicans. *Political Science Quarterly* 109(4): 571–593.

Constantini, Edmond. 1990. Political Women and Political Ambition: Closing the Gender Gap. *American Journal of Political Science* 34: 741–770.

Conway, M. Margaret, Gertrude A. Steuernagel, and David W. Ahern. 1997. *Women and Political Participation*. Washington, D.C.: Congressional Quarterly Press.

Cook, Elizabeth A., Sue Thomas, and Clyde Wilcox, eds. 1994. *The Year of the Woman: Myths and Realities*. Boulder: Westview.

Cox, Gary W. and Matthew D. McCubbins. 1993. *Legislative Leviathan: Party Government in the House*. Berkeley: University of California Press.

Crawford, M. and M. MacLeod. 1990. Gender in the College Classroom: An Assessment of the "Chilly Climate" for Women. *Sex Roles* 23: 101–122.

Darcy, R., Susan Welch, and Janet Clark. 1994. *Women, Elections, and Representation*. Lincoln: University of Nebraska Press.

Deckard, Barbara. 1976. Electoral Marginality and Party Loyalty in House Roll Call Voting. *American Journal of Political Science* 20(3): 469–482.

Dodson, Debra L. 1998. Representing Women's Interests in the U.S. House of Representatives. In *Women and Elective Office: Past, Present, and Future*, eds. Sue Thomas and Clyde Wilcox. Oxford: Oxford University Press.

Dodson, Debra L. and Susan J. Carroll. 1991. *Reshaping the Agenda: Women in State Legislatures*. New Brunswick: Center for the American Woman and Politics, Rutgers, The State University of New Jersey.

Dolan, Kathleen. 1998. Voting for Women in the Year of the Woman. *American Journal of Political Science* 42: 272–293.

Drass, K. A. 1986. The Effect of Gender Identity on Conversation. *Social Psychology Quarterly* 49: 294–301.

Duerst-Lahti, G. 2002. Knowing Congress as a Gendered Institution: Manliness and the Implications of Women in Congress. In *Women Transforming Congress*, ed. Cindy S. Rosenthal. Norman, OK: University of Oklahoma Press.

Dye, Thomas. 1961. A Comparison of Constituency Influences in the Upper and Lower Chambers of a State Legislature. *Western Political Quarterly* 14: 473–480.

Eakins, Barbara Westbrook. 1978. *Sex Differences in Human Communication*. Boston: Houghton Mifflin.

Eldersveld, Samuel J. 1964. *Political Parties*. Chicago: Rand McNally.

Elving, Ronald. June 11, 1988. Debating Length, Language, Democrats Ponder Platform. *CQ Weekly Report* 1583.

Erikson, Robert S. 1971. The Electoral Impact of Congressional Roll Call Voting. *American Political Science Review* 65: 1018–1032.

Evans, C. Lawrence and Walter J. Oleszek. 1999. Procedural Features of House Republican Rule. In *New Majority or Old Minority?: The Impact of Republicans on Congress*, eds. Nicol C. Rae and Colton C. Campbell. Lanham, MD: Rowman & Littlefield.

Fenno, Richard F., Jr. 1973. *Congressmen in Committees*. Boston: Little, Brown.

———. 1977. U.S. House Members in Their Constituencies: An Exploration. *American Political Science Review* 71: 883–917.

———. 1978. *Home Style: House Members and Their Districts*. Boston: Little, Brown.

———. 1990. *Watching Politicians: Essays on Participant Observation*. Berkeley, CA: IGS Press.

———. 1999. U.S. House Members in Their Constituencies: An Exploration. Reprinted in *Classics in Congressional Politics*, eds. Herbert F. Weisberg, Eric S. Heberlig, and Lisa M. Campoli. New York: Longman.

Fiorina, Morris P. 1977. *Congress: Keystone of the Washington Establishment.* New Haven, Conn.: Yale University Press.

———. 1974. *Representatives, Roll Calls, and Constituencies.* Lexington, MA: D.C. Heath.

Flinn, Thomas A. 1964. Party Responsibility in the States: Some Casual Factors. *American Political Science Review* 58: 60–72.

Forgette, Richard. 2002. Congressional Part Congressional Party Building: The Practice of Partisanship. Paper prepared for presentation at the annual meeting of the Midwest Political Science Association. Chicago, Illinois: April 25–28, 2002.

Fowler, Linda L. and Robert McClure. 1989. *Political Ambition.* New Haven: Yale University Press.

Fowlkes, Diane. L., Jerry Perkins, and Sue T. Rinehart. 1979. Gender Roles and Party Roles. *The American Political Science Review* 73: 772–780.

Fox, Richard L. 1997. *Gender Dynamics in Congressional Elections.* Thousand Oaks: Sage.

Fox, Richard L., Jennifer L. Lawless, and Courtney Feeley. 2001. Gender and the Decision to Run for Office. *Legislative Studies Quarterly* 26(3): 411–435.

Freeman, Jo Ann. 1986. The Political Culture of the Democratic and Republican Parties. *Political Science Quarterly* 101(3): 327–356.

———. 2000. *A Room at a Time: How Women Entered Party Politics.* Lanham, MD: Rowman and Littlefield.

Froman, Lewis A. 1963. *Congressmen and Their Constituencies.* Chicago: McNally.

Froman, Lewis and Randall Ripley. 1965. Conditions for Party Leadership. *American Political Science Review* 59: 52–63.

Gaddie, Ronald K. and Charles S. Bullock, III. 2000. *Elections to Open Seats in the House: Where the Action Is.* Lanham, MD: Rowman and Littlefield.

Gertzog, Irwin N. 1976. The Routinization of Committee Assignments in the U.S. House of Representatives. *American Journal of Political Science* 20(4): 693–712.

Gilmour, John B. and Paul Rothstein. 1993. Early Republican Retirement: A Cause of Democratic Dominance in the House of Representatives. *Legislative Studies Quarterly* 18: 345–365.

Gimple, J. G. 1996. *Fulfilling the Contract: The First 100 Days.* Needham Heights, MA: Allyn & Bacon.

Goodwin, George, Jr. 1959. The Seniority System in Congress. *The American Political Science Review* 53(2): 412–436.

Green, Philip. 1992. A Few Kind Words for Liberalism. *Nation* 255: 324–329.

Hale, Jon F. 1995. The Making of the New Democrats. *Political Science Quarterly* 110(2): 207–232.

Hale, M. 1999. He Says, She Says: Gender and Worklife. *Public Administration Review* 59(5): 410–424.

Hale, M. 1992. New Politics Liberals and DLC Centrists: Factionalism in the Democratic Party, 1968–1992. Paper delivered at the annual meeting of the American Political Science Association, Chicago, IL.

Hall, Richard L. 1996. *Participation in Congress.* New Haven: Yale University Press.

———. 1992. Measuring Legislative Influence. *Legislative Studies Quarterly* 17: 205–232.

Hall, Richard L. and C. Lawrence Evans. 1990. The Power of Subcommittees. *The Journal of Politics* 52(2): 335–355.

Hoffman, Kim, Carrie Palmer, and Ronald K. Gaddie. 2001. Candidate Sex and Congressional Elections Outcomes: A Longitudinal Look Through the Open Seats. In *Women and Congress: Running, Winning, and Ruling*, ed. Karen O'Connor. New York: Haworth.

Huckfeldt, Robert and Carol Kohfeld. 1989. *Race and the Decline of Class in American Politics*. Urbana: The University of Illinois Press.

Huitt, Ralph. 1961. Democratic Party Leadership in the Senate. *American Political Science Review* 55: 333–344.

Huntington, Samuel P. 1950. A Revised Theory of American Party Politics. *American Political Science Review* 44: 669–677.

Ippolito, Dennis S. and Thomas G. Walker. 1980. *Political Parties, Interest Groups, and Public Policy: Group Influence in American Politics*. Englewood Cliffs, NJ: Prentice-Hall, Inc.

Jacobson, Gary C. 1997. *The Politics of Congressional Elections*, 4th ed. New York: Longman.

———. 1987. The Marginals Never Vanished: Incumbency and Competition in Elections to the U.S. House of Representatives, 1952–82. *American Journal of Political Science* 31(1): 126–141.

Jacobson, Gary C. and Samuel Kernell. 1983. *Strategy and Choice in Congressional Elections*, 2nd ed. New Haven: Yale University Press.

———. 1999. Strategic Politicians. Reprinted in *Classics in Congressional Politics*, eds. Herbert F. Weisberg, Eric S. Heberlig, and Lisa M. Campoli. New York: Longman.

Jennings, M. Kent and Barbara G. Farah. 1981. Social Roles and Political Resources: An Over-Time Study of Men and Women in Party Elites. *American Journal of Political Science* 25(3): 462–482.

Jewell, Malcolm. 1955. Party Voting in American State Legislatures. *American Political Science Review* 49: 773–791.

Jewell, Malcolm and Samuel Patterson. 1966. *The Legislative Process in the United States*. New York: Random House.

Kahn, Kim F. 1996. *The Political Consequences of Being a Woman*. New York: Columbia University Press.

Kanter, R. M. 1977. *Men and Women of the Corporation*. New York: Basic Books.

Kathlene, Lyn. 1995. Position Power versus Gender Power: Who Holds the Floor? In *Gender Power, Leadership, and Governance*, eds. G. Duerst-Lahti and R. M. Kelly. Ann Arbor: University of Michigan Press.

———. 1994. Power and Influence in State Legislative Policy Making: The Interaction of Gender and Power in Committee Hearing Debates. *American Political Science Review* 88(3): 560–576.

Kenney, S. 1997. New Research on Gendered Political Institutions. *Political Research Quarterly* 49(2): 445–466.

Kirkpatrick, Jeane. 1976. *The New Presidential Elite*. New York: Russell Sage Foundation and the Twentieth Century Fund.

Koetzle, William. 1998. The Impact of Constituency Diversity upon the Competitiveness of U.S. House of Representatives Elections, 1962–96. *Legislative Studies Quarterly* 23(November): 561–574.

Kollock, Peter, Philip Blumstein, and Pepper Schwartz. 1985. Sex and Power in Interaction: Conversational Privileges and Duties. *American Sociological Review* 50: 34–47.

Krasno, Jonathan S. *Challengers, Competition, and Reelection: Comparing Senate and House Elections.* New Haven: Yale University Press.

Kuklinski, James H. 1977. District Competitiveness and Legislative Roll-Call Behavior: A Reassessment of the Marginality Hypothesis. *American Journal of Political Science* 21(3): 627–638.

Lakoff, Robin T. 1990. *Talking Power: The Politics of Language in Our Lives.* New York: Basic Books.

Leader, Shelah G. 1977. The Policy Impact of Elected Women Officials. In *The Impact of the Electoral Process*, eds. Joseph Cooper and Louis Maisels. Beverly Hills: Sage.

Leeper, Mark. 1991. The Impact of Prejudice on Female Candidates: An Experimental Look at Voter Inference. *American Politics Quarterly* 19: 248–261.

Leet-Pellegrini, H. M. 1980. Conversational Dominance as a Function of Gender and Expertise. In *Language: Social Psychological Perspectives*, eds. H. Giles, W. P. Robinson, and P. M. Smith. Oxford: Pergamon.

Levy, Mark and Kramer, Michael. 1976. *The Ethnic Factor.* New York: Simon and Schuster.

Loomis, Burdett A. Congressional Careers and Party Leadership in the Contemporary House of Representatives. *American Journal of Political Science* 28(1): 180–202.

Lowry, William R. and Charles R. Shipan. 2002. Party Differentiation in Congress. *Legislative Studies Quarterly* 27(1): 33–60.

MacRae, Duncan, Jr. 1958. *Dimensions of Congressional Voting.* Berkeley: University of California Press: 284–289.

———. 1952. The Relation Between Roll Call Votes and Constituencies in the Massachusetts House of Representatives. *American Political Science Review* 46: 1046–1055.

Masters, Nicholas A. 1961. Committee Assignments in the House of Representatives. *American Political Science Review* 55(2): 345–357.

Mattei, Laura R. W. 1998. Gender and Power in American Legislative Discourse. *The Journal of Politics* 60(2): 440–461.

Mayhew, David, R. 1974a. *Congress: The Electoral Connection.* New Haven, Co.: Yale University Press.

———. 1974b. Congressional Elections: The Case of the Vanishing Marginals. *Polity* 6: 295–317.

———. 1999. Congressional Elections: The Case of the Vanishing Marginals. Reprinted in *Classics in Congressional Politics*, eds. Herbert F. Weisberg, Eric S. Heberlig, and Lisa M. Campoli. New York: Longman.

McDermott, Monika L. 1997. Voting Cues in Low-Information Elections: Candidate Gender as a Social Information Variable in Contemporary United States Elections. *American Journal of Political Science* 41(1): 270–283.

Miller, K. C. 1995. Will These Women Clean House? *Policy Review* 72: 77–80.

Miller, Warren E. and J. Merrill Shanks. 1996. *The New American Voter.* Cambridge, MA: Harvard University Press.

Miller, Warren E. and Donald E. Stokes. 1963. Constituency Influence in Congress. *American Political Science Review* 57: 45–57.

———. 1999. Constituency Influence in Congress. Reprinted in *Classics in Congressional Politics*, eds. Herbert F. Weisberg, Eric S. Heberlig, and Lisa M. Campoli. New York: Longman.

Moore, Michael K. and John R. Hibbing. 1998. Situational Dissatisfaction in Congress: Explaining Voluntary Departures. *The Journal of Politics* 60(4): 1088–1107.

Monroe, J. P. 2001. *The Political Party Matrix: The Persistence of Organization*. Albany, NY: SUNY Press.

Moore, Michael K. and John R. Hibbing. 1998. Situational Dissatisfaction in Congress: Explaining Voluntary Departures. *The Journal of Politics* 60(4): 1088–1107.

National Women's Political Caucus (NWPC). 1994. *Why Don't More Women Run? A Study Prepared by Mellman, Lazarus, and Lake*. Washington, D.C.: National Women's Political Caucus.

Norton, Noelle. 2002. Transforming Policy from the Inside: Participation in Committee. In *Women Transforming Congress*, ed. Cindy S. Rosenthal. Norman, OK: University of Oklahoma Press.

———. 1999. Uncovering the Dimensionality of Gender Voting in Congress. *Legislative Studies Quarterly* 24(1): 65–86.

Ornstein, Norman J., Thomas E. Mann, and Michael J. Malbin. 1994. *Vital Statistics on Congress 1993–1994*. Washington, D.C.: CQ Press.

Ornstein, Norman J. and Amy L. Schenkenberg. 1995. The 1995 Congress: The First Hundred Days and Beyond. *Political Science Quarterly* 110(2): 183–206.

Owens, John E. 1997. The Return of Party Government in the US House of Representatives: Central Leadership–Committee Relations in the 104th Congress. *British Journal of Political Science* 27(2): 247–272.

Parker, Glenn R. 1992. *Institutional Change, Discretion, and the Making of Modern Congress: An Economic Interpretation*. Ann Arbor, MI: University of Michigan.

———. 1996. *Congress and the Rent-Seeking Society*. Ann Arbor, MI: University of Michigan.

Peabody, Robert L. 1976. *Leadership in Congress: Stability, Succession, and Change*. Boston, MA: Little, Brown.

Peters, Ronald M., Jr. 2002. Caucus and Conference: Party Organization in the U.S. House of Representatives. Paper prepared for presentation at the annual meeting of the Midwest Political Science Association. Chicago, Illinois: April 25–28, 2002.

Pinney, Neil and George Serra. 1999. The Congressional Black Caucus and Vote Cohesion: Placing the Caucus within House Voting Patterns. *Political Research Quarterly* 52(3): 583–608.

Plutzer, Eric and John E. Zipp. 1996. Identity Politics, Partisanship, and Voting for Women Candidates. *The Public Opinion Quarterly* 6(1): 30–57.

Polsby, Nelson W., Miriam Gallager, and Barry S. Rundquist. 1969. The Growth of the Seniority System in the U.S. House of Representatives. *American Political Science Review* 63: 787–807.

Pomper, G. M. 1985. The Nominations. In *The Election of 1984: Reports and Interpretations*, ed. Gerald M. Pomper. Chatham, NJ: Chatham House.

———. 1972. From Confusion to Clarity: Issues and American Voters, 1956–1968. *American Political Science Review* 66: 415–428.

———. 1971. Toward a More Responsible Two-Party System: What, Again? *The Journal of Politics* 33: 916–940.

Poole, Keith T. 2000. Description of Nominate Data. Keith Poole's website (http://voteview.uh.edu/page2a.htm).

Poole, Keith T. and Howard Rosenthal. 1997. *Congress: A Political-Economic History of Roll Call Voting*. New York: Oxford University Press.

———. 1991. Patterns of Congressional Voting. *American Journal of Political Science* 35(1): 228–278.

———. 1985. A Spatial Model for Legislative Roll Call Analysis. *American Journal of Political Science* 29(2): 357–384.

Putnam, Robert D. 1993. *Making Democracy Work: Civic Traditions in Modern Italy*. Princeton, NJ: Princeton University Press.

Ridgeway, Cecilia L. and Carhryn Johnson. 1990. What is the Relationship Between Socioemotional Behavior and Status in Task Groups? *American Journal of Sociology* 95: 1189–1212.

Riley, Russell. 1995. Party Government and the Contract with America. *PS: Political Science and Politics* 28(4): 703–707.

Ripley, Randall B. 1967. *Party Leaders in the House of Representatives*. Washington, D.C.: Brookings Institution.

Rohde, David. 1991. *Parties and Leaders in the Postreform House*. Chicago: University of Chicago Press.

———. 1999. Risk-Bearing and Progressive Ambition: The Case of Members of the U.S. House of Representatives. Reprinted in *Classics in Congressional Politics*, eds. Herbert F. Weisberg, Eric S. Heberlig, and Lisa M. Campoli. New York: Longman, 1999.

———. 1991. *Parties and Leaders in the Postreform House*. Chicago: University of Chicago Press.

———. 1979. Risk Bearing and Progressive Ambition. *American Journal of Political Science* 23: 1–26.

———. 1974. Committee Reform in the House of Representatives and the Subcommittee Bill of Rights. *The Annals* 411: 39–47.

Rohde, David W. and Kenneth A. Shepsle. 1973. Democratic Committee Assignments in the House of Representatives: Strategic Aspects of a Social Choice Process. *The American Political Science Review* 67(3): 889–905.

Rosenthal, Cindy S. 1998. *When Women Lead: Integrative Leadership in State Legislative Committees*. New York: Oxford University Press.

Roukema, Marge. 2001. Roukema Statement on Banking Committee Chairmanship. 2469 Rayburn House Office Building Washington, D.C. 20515: Press Release, Office of Marge Roukema.

Sacks, H., E. Schegloff, and G. Jefferson. 1974. A Simplest Systematics for the Organization of Turn-taking for Conversation. *Language* 50: 696–735.

Saint-Germain, M. A. 1989. Does Their Difference Make a Difference? The Impact of Women on Public Policy in the Arizona Legislature. *Social Science Quarterly* 70: 956–968.

Schattschneider, E. E. 1942. *Party Government*. New York: Rinehart.

Schlesinger, Arthur M., Jr. 1990. The Liberal Opportunity. *American Prospect* 1: 10–18.

Schlozman, Kay L., Nancy Burns, Sidney Verba, and Jesse Donahue. 1995. Gender and Citizen Participation: Is There a Different Voice? *American Journal of Political Science* 39(2): 267–293.

Schwindt, L. A. 2000. The Effects of Gender Turnover on Ideological Change in the House of Representatives. Paper prepared for presentation at the University of Oklahoma Carl Albert Congressional Research and Studies Center conference "Women Transforming Congress: Gender Analyses of Institutional Life." April 13–15, 2000.

Seltzer, Richard A., Jody Newman, and Melissa V. Leighton. 1997. *Sex as a Political Variable*. Boulder. CO: Lynne Reinner.

Shafer, Byron E. 1988. *Bifurcated Politics*. Cambridge, MA: Harvard University Press.

Shannon, Wayne W. 1968a. *Party, Constituency and Congressional Voting*. Baton Rouge, LA: Louisiana State University Press.

———. 1968b. Electoral Margins and Voting Behavior in the House of Representatives: The Case of the Eighty-Sixth and Eighty-Seventh Congresses. *Journal of Politics* 30(4): 1028–1045.

Sinclair, Barbara. 1999. Partisan Imperatives and Institutional Constraints: Republican Party Leadership in the House and Senate. In *New Majority or Old Minority?: The Impact of Republicans on Congress*, eds. Nicol C. Rae and Colton C. Campbell. Lanham, MD: Rowman & Littlefield.

———. 1995. *Legislators, Leaders, and Lawmaking: The U.S. House of Representatives in the Postreform Era*. Baltimore, MD: Johns Hopkins University Press.

———. 1983. *Majority Leadership in the U.S. House*. Baltimore, MD: Johns Hopkins University Press.

Smith, Steven S. 2000. Positive Theories of Congressional Parties. *Legislative Studies Quarterly* 25(2): 193–215.

Smith-Lovin, Lynn and Dawn T. Robinson. 1992. Gender and Conversational Dynamics. In *Gender, Interaction, and Inequality*, ed. Cecilia L. Ridgeway. New York: Springer-Verlag.

Sullivan, John L. and Eric M. Uslaner. 1978. Congressional Behavior and Electoral Marginality. *American Journal of Political Science* 22(3): 536–553.

Swann, J. 1988. Talk Control: An Illustration from the Classroom of Problems in Analyzing Male Dominance of Conversation. In *Women in Their Speech Communities*, eds. Jennifer Coates and Deborah Cameron. London: Longman.

Swers, Michele L. 2002. *The Difference Women Make: The Policy Impact of Women in Congress*. Chicago: University of Chicago Press.

———. 2002. Transforming the Agenda: Analyzing Gender Differences in Women's Issue Bill Sponsorship. In *Women Transforming Congress*, ed. Cindy S. Rosenthal. Norman, OK: University of Oklahoma Press.

———. 1998. Are Women More Likely to Vote for Women's Issue Bills than Their Male Colleagues? *Legislative Studies Quarterly* 23(3): 435–448.

Tamerius, K. L. 1995. Sex, Gender, and Leadership in the Representation of Women. In *Gender Power, Leadership, and Governance*, eds. Georgia Duerst-Lahti and Rita Mae Kelly. Ann Arbor, MI: University of Michigan Press.

Theriault, Sean. 1998. Moving Up or Moving Out: Career Ceilings and Congressional Retirement. *Legislative Studies Quarterly* 23: 419–433.

Thomas, Sue. 1998. Introduction: Women and Elective Office: Past, Present, and Future. In *Women and Elective Office*, eds. Sue Thomas and Clyde Wilcox. New York: Oxford University Press.

———. 1994. *How Women Legislate.* New York: Oxford University Press.

Thomas, Sue and Susan Welch. 1991. The Impact of Women on State Legislative Policies. *The Journal of Politics* 53(4): 958–976.

Thomas, Sue and Clyde Wilcox, eds. 1998. *Women and Elective Office.* New York: Oxford University Press.

Uhlaner, Carole and Kay Lehman Schlozman. 1986. Candidate Gender and Congressional Campaign Receipts. *Journal of Politics* 48: 30–50.

Van Dyke, Vernon. 1995. *Ideology and Political Choice: The Search for Freedom, Justice, and Virtue.* Chatham, NJ: Chatham House Publishers, Inc.

Vega, A. and Juanita M. Firestone. 1995. The Effects of Gender on Congressional Behavior and the Substantive Representation of Women. *Legislative Studies Quarterly* 20(2): 213–222.

Waldman, Sidney. 1980. Majority Leadership in the House of Representatives. *Political Science Quarterly* 95(3): 373–393.

Walsh, Katherine C. 2002. Enlarging Representation: Women Bringing Marginalized Perspectives to Floor Debate in the House of Representatives. In *Women Transforming Congress*, ed. Cindy S. Rosenthal. Norman, OK: University of Oklahoma Press.

Wattenberg, Martin P. 1998. *The Decline of American Political Parties, 1952–1996.* Cambridge, MA: Harvard University Press.

Weisber, Herbert F., Eric S. Heberlig, and Lisa M. Campoli, eds. 1999. *Classics in Congressional Politics.* New York: Longman.

Welch, Susan. 1985. Are Women More Liberal than Men in the U.S. Congress? *Legislative Studies Quarterly* 10(1): 125–134.

Wilhite, Allen and John Thielmann. 1986. Women, Blacks, and PAC Discrimination. *Social Science Quarterly* 67: 283–298.

Williams, Clare B. (Assistant Chairman, RNC). 1962. *The History of the Founding and Development of the National Federation of Republican Women.* Washington, D.C.: Republican National Committee.

Wolbrecht, Christina. 2002. Female Legislators and the Women's Rights Agenda: From Feminine Mystique to Feminist Era. In *Women Transforming Congress*, ed. Cindy S. Rosenthal. Norman, OK: University of Oklahoma Press.

Wolfinger, Raymond E. and Steven J. Rosenstone. 1980. *Who Votes?* New York: Yale University Press.

Yoder, Janice D. 1991. Rethinking Tokenism: Looking Beyond Numbers. *Gender and Sociology* 5: 178–192.

Zimmerman, Don H. and Candace West. 1975. Sex Roles, Interruptions and Silences in Conversations. In *Language and Sex: Difference and Dominance*, eds. B. Thorne and N. Henley. Rowley, MA: Newbury House.

Zipp, John F. and Eric Plutzer. 1985. Gender Differences in Voting for Female Candidates: Evidence From the 1982 Election. *The Public Opinion Quarterly* 49(2): 179–197.

Index

agenda
  domestic policy, 106
  foreign policy, 106
Ahern, David W., 28
Aistrup, Joseph, 35
Aldrich, John H., 7–8, 13
ambition, 17, 26, 33, 37, 128, 130, 136
American Conservative Union, The
      (ACU), 54, 60
Americans for Democratic Action
      (ADA), 54, 60–61
Andres, Gary J., 8–9
Ansolabehere, Stephen, 120
antifeminist, 59
Armey, Richard, 8, 136
Asians, 10
Assistant to the House Democratic
      Leader, 99

backgrounds, 28, 30–31, 33–34,
      127–128
Baer, Denise, 5
Bales, Robert F., 89
Banking Committee, 1, 79
Berelson, Bernard, 35
Bernick, F. Lee, 136
Bianco, William T., 23, 64
Biersack, Robert, 27
bipartisanship, 16
Blacks, 10
Bledsoe, Timothy, 26
Blue Dogs, 114, 135
Bond, Jon R., 23, 64
Brady, David W., 88
Brandes Crook, Sara, 83

Bullock, Charles S., III, 27, 30
Burrell, Barbara, 27
Bush, George W., 31, 42
business, 10

camaraderie, 109–111, 116
Camp, Dave, 116
campaign, 101–102, 114
  activities, 26
  fundraising, 34, 47
Campaign Committee, 94–95, 97
Campbell, A., 35
Cannon, Joe, 8
Canon, David T., 23, 64
Cantor, D. M., 54–55
career, 128, 135–136
Carroll, Susan J., 26
Center for American Women and
      Politics (CAWP), 33–34
children, 115
Clark, Janet, 26–27
Clinton, Bill, 42
collective action
  problem of, 81
committee, 8
  assignments, 81–82
  assignments and party
        culture, 82
  assignments and seniority, 83
  chairmanships, 83
  chairs, 83, 99, 118, 130
  chairs and party unity, 83
  leadership structure, 99, 130
  prestigious assignments, 83
Committee on Committees, 82

Committee on Merchant Marine and Fisheries
  chair of, 99
Committee on Political Parties (1950), 8
Committee on Small Business
  chair of, 99
Committee on Veteran's Affairs
  chair of, 99
competitive districts, 23
Congress, 103rd, 2, 4, 8, 15, 40, 43–44, 64, 70, 72, 90–91, 94–96, 98, 120
Congress, 104th, 2, 8, 15, 38, 41–42, 44, 46, 55, 70, 72, 94–96, 98–99, 120–121
Congress, 105th, 38, 64, 70, 94–96, 98, 120, 136
Congress, 106th, 33, 64, 68, 70, 72, 94, 96, 98, 136
Congress 107th, 2, 4, 6–7, 15, 22, 43–44, 46, 60–61, 70, 79, 88, 90–91, 94–96, 98, 135
Congress: The Electoral Connection, 22
congressional arena, 17
Congressional Black Caucus, 10, 135
Congressional Delegation (CODEL), 1, 116
Congressional Quarterly, 54
Connelly, William F., 25
consensus
  building, 112, 119
conservative women, 25, 38, 57, 59
Constantini, Edmond, 26
constituency
  centered model, 129, 134
  responsiveness, 18, 46
Contract with America, 8
Converse, P. E., 35
Conway, M. Margaret, 28
Cook, Elizabeth A., 26
Cox, Gary W., 6, 123
Crawford, M., 89
credibility, 33

Darcy, R., 26–27
data, 126
database, 11
dataset, 4, 15
Deckard, Barbara, 23
delegate selection process, 10
Democratic
  organizational style, 87
  representational ethos, 87
  voting behavior, 65–68
Democratic Caucus, 16, 88, 100, 110, 114, 121, 130, 135
  organizational context, 84–85
Democratic Chief Deputy Whip, 99
Democratic Congressional Campaign Committee (DCCC), 54
  Chair of, 99
Democratic National Committee, 10
Democratic Party, 24–25, 27, 90
Democratic Women's Caucus, 113
decision to run, 28
discretion, 3, 12, 35, 47–48, 74, 125–126, 128, 130, 134
district
  diversity thesis, 35
  heterogeneity, 35
Dodson, Debra L., 26
Dolan, Kathleen, 56
Duerst-Lahti, G., 56–57
Dunn, Jennifer, 136
DW-NOMINATE, 42–45, 54, 60–72, 75
Dye, Thomas, 88

Eakins, Barbara Westbrook, 89
Eldersveld, Samuel J., 53–54
electoral
  arena, 17
  "connection," 81
  constraints, 38, 119, 130
  incentive, 47
  pressures, 3, 19, 48, 53, 76, 80, 81, 100, 119

returns, 39
security, 12–14, 19, 22–23, 40, 44,
    68, 132
vulnerability, 66, 70
electorate, 19
Elving, Ronald, 10
endorsement, 31–32
Erikson, Robert S., 23
exclusive committees, 94–96, 98
expertise, 112

factor analysis, 63, 107
family, 28, 38, 115, 127
    responsibilities, 115
Farah, Barbara G., 58
Feeley, Courtney, 26–27
female
    representation, 27, 118, 132
    Republican Members, 70
    vote, 27
feminalism, 57
feminist movement, 55, 57–59
Fenno, Richard F., Jr., 4, 6, 12, 15, 17,
    22, 47, 120, 127
Fiorina, Morris P., 22–23, 35, 47
Firestone, Juanita M., 51, 55
Flinn, Thomas A., 88
Forbes, Randy, 101
Forgette, Richard, 86
Fowler, Linda L., 26
Fox, Richard L., 26, 28
Freeman, Jo Ann, 7, 10, 23, 86–87
Froman, Lewis A., 23, 35
full committee chair, 98
fundraising
    campaign, 81
    national, 100, 102–103, 109

Gaddie, Ronald K., 27
gays, 10
gender
    composition, 90–91
    critics of theory, 55
    differences, 12, 15

gendered, 5, 12, 26, 57
socialization, 5
stereotypes, 26–27, 127
theory, 2, 5–6, 55–57, 75, 89,
    101, 134
Gephardt, Richard, 1
Gimpel, J. G., 55
Gingrich, Newt, 7–9, 83
goal motivations, 6, 13
goal
    orientations, 7
goals, 124–126, 128
Gonzalez, Elian, 106
GOP, 31, 42, 55
Granger, Kay, 116

Hale, M., 10–11
Hall, Richard L., 16, 127
Hastert, Dennis, 9, 110
Hays, Patricia Lee Findley, 30
Herring, Mary, 26
Herrnson, Paul S., 27, 54–55
Hibbing, John R., 83, 121, 136
Hispanics, 10
Homestyle, 22
House Democratic Caucus
    see also Democratic Caucus
    Secretary of, 98
House Democratic Whip,
    99, 130
House Majority Leader, 136
House Republican Conference, 16,
    110, 130
    see also Republican Conference
    meetings, 101
    organizational context, 84
    Secretary of, 99
    Vice Chair of, 99
Huckfeldt, Robert, 35
Huntington, Samuel P., 23

ideological
    character, 23, 61
    compromise, 112

ideological—*continued*
  homogeneity, 18, 25
  voting behavior, 18
ideology, 34, 41, 43, 46, 52–53, 57
inclusion, 76
incumbency advantage, 12
institution, 19, 89
institutional identities, 86
interview data, 4, 15, 17
intrusiveness theory, 90
Ippolito, Dennis S., 53–54
issue framing, 58

Jacobson, Gary C., 34
Jennings, M. Kent, 58
Jewell, Malcolm, 88
Johnson, Cathryn, 89
Johnson, Nancy, 99

Kahn, Kim F., 26
Kanter, R. M., 90
Kathlene, Lyn, 5, 89–90
Kelly, Sue, 116
Kenney, S., 89
key votes, 54
Kirkpatrick, Jeane, 54
Koetzle, William, 35
Kohfeld, Carol, 35
Kramer, Michael, 35
Kuklinski, James H., 23

Largent, Steve, 136
Lawless, Jennifer L., 26–27
Lazarsfeld, Paul, 35
Leader, Shelah G., 51
leadership, 8–9, 37–38, 47, 88, 91,
    103–104, 113–114, 118–119,
    124–126, 129–130, 135
  Democratic, 29
  formal position, 107
  structure, 94–96, 98
  team, 91, 94–95, 97, 106
Leeper, Mark, 27
Leet-Pellegrini, H.M., 89

"legislative cartel," 81
Leighton, Melissa V., 27
Levy, Mark, 35
liberal
  ideology scores, 100
liberals, 10
Livingston, Robert, 7

MacLeod, M., 89
MacRae, Duncan, Jr., 23, 88
majority status, 19
marginality, 34–36, 40–41, 46, 65, 71,
    106, 132
  thesis, 23
  party support, 82
Mattei, Laura R. W., 90
Mayhew, David R., 6, 12, 22, 34, 47
McCarthy, Carolyn, 28
McClure, Robert, 26
McCubbins, Matthew D., 6, 123
McDermott, Monika L., 128
McPhee, William, 35
media, 100, 105–107, 109, 113, 129
mediating institutions, 126
Member goals, 7
Meyers, Jan, 99
Miller, W. E., 35, 53, 23, 35, 132
minority status, 56
Moore, Michael K., 121, 136
motivations, 22
multiple measures, 127
Myers, Jon, 7
Myrick, Sue, 116

National Democratic Club Public
    Policy Committee, 11
National Federation of Republican
    Women, 16
National Federation of Women's
    Republican Clubs (NFWRC), 9
National Journal, The, 54, 60–61
*National Journal's Almanac of American
    Politics, The (1994–2002)*, 15
national political media, 99

National Republican Campaign Committee (NRCC), 16, 31–33, 37
National Women's Political Caucus (NWPC), 26
New Democrats, 135
Newman, Jody, 27
Norton, Noelle, 56

organizational
    attendance, 100
    context, 84
    context and structure, 84
    context and administration, 84
    records, 100
    style, 24, 87
Ornstein, Norman J., 38
Owens, John E., 7–9

Parker, Glenn R., 12, 47, 131
partial-birth abortion, 58
participant observer, 4, 15
participation, 90, 100, 103, 127, 131
participatory homogeneity, 13
partisan arena, 17, 22
partisanship, 12, 123
party
    affiliation, 15
    collective goals, 80
    culture, 24, 46–47, 86
    Democratic culture, 10–11, 18, 48, 74
    disloyalty, 23
    elites, 32, 54, 57–58, 127
    incentives, 81
    leaders, 80
    leadership, 81–82
    leadership and party unity, 84
    leadership theory, 104
    loyalty, 9, 17
    organizations, 19, 80, 85
    Republican culture, 7, 9, 18, 27, 74
    resources, 81
    role of women, 87

spending and party unity scores, 86
theory, 7, 9, 16, 85, 110–111, 120, 125, 127, 129, 134,
thesis, 10–11, 13, 19, 74–75, 132
unity, 3, 54, 72–73, 76, 88, 100, 107–111
party-building activities, 18, 85–86, 100, 102–104, 106–107, 109, 119, 129–130, 132
    communications, 85
Patterson, Samuel, 88
Pelosi, Nancy, 1, 88, 102, 124, 130
personal interviews, 11, 16, 126–127
perspectives, 58
Peters, Ronald M., Jr., 84–85, 88
Pinney, Neil, 10
pioneer, 111, 129
Pitney, John J., Jr., 25
Plutzer, Eric, 27, 127
polarization, 43
Policy and Steering Committees, 79, 94–95, 97, 129
Political Action Committee (PAC), 3, 18, 99, 102–104, 106–107
political experience, 31
Politics in America, 90
Polsby, Nelson W., 88
Pomper, G. M., 11
Poole, Keith T., 42, 54, 60–61, 75
presidential vote return, 23, 40, 42, 63–64
principal-agent
    relationship, 130
    theory, 74
Progressive Caucus, 135
Progressives, 114
protoideology, 57
Pryce, Deborah, 1, 57, 89, 130

qualitative data, 22
quantitative data, 15–16

ranking
    member of subcommittee, 94, 98

ranking—*continued*
  positions, 95
  positions on committees, 103
rational choice theory, 35, 132
recruitment, 32–33
reelection, 12–13, 17, 21, 81, 124
reforms, 8–9, 81, 83
Regula, Ralph, 7
representation, 24
  unitary conception of, 87
  minority coalition-building
    conception of, 87
reproductive
  rights, 56
  policy, 56
Republican
  leadership, 79
  organizational style, 87
  representational ethos, 87
  voting behavior, 66, 68–69, 71
Republican Conference, 1, 101
Republican Convention (1996), 121
Republican National Committee
    (RNC), 30–32
Republican Party, 24–25, 90
  sponsorship, 87
Republican Women's Task Force of
    the National Women's Political
    Caucus (RWTF), 87
responsible party model, 8,
    129, 134
"Retain Our Majority Party" (ROMP)
    List, 37
Ridgeway, Cecilia L., 89
Riley, Russell, 8
Robinson, Dawn T., 89
Rogers, Edith Nourse, 99
Rohde, David, 6, 88, 123
  Aldrich and, 7–8, 13
role, 112–113
Rosenstone, Steven J., 35
Rosenthal, Howard, 42, 54,
    60–61, 75
Ros-Lehtinen, Ileana, 106

Roukema, Marge, 1, 79, 135–136
  Banking Committee, 1, 135
routes to office, 29

Schenkenberg, Amy L., 38
Schlozman, Kay L., 89, 102
Schwindt, L. A., 51, 55
Seltzer, Richard A., 27
seniority, 125, 132
  rule, 7, 13–15, 48, 125–126, 129,
    135–136
September 11, 2001, 16
Shafer, Byron E., 10
Shanks, J. Merrill, 53
Shannon, Wayne W., 23
Sinclair, Barbara, 6, 123
Sisisky, Norman, 101
Smith-Lovin, Lynn, 89
social
  "capital," 86
  identity, 124
  issues, 3, 5, 36, 60, 62, 64, 74, 76,
    128–129
  liberalism, 70
  ratings, 66, 70
Speaker, 111, 113
State of the Union, 136
status, 125, 130
Steuernagel, Gertrude A., 28
Stokes, D. E., 35
"Subcommittee Bill of Rights," 83
subcommittee chairs, 94, 96
Sullivan, John L., 23
Sullivan, Leonor, 99
Swers, Michele L., 3, 6, 12, 51, 56,
    123, 136
swing district, 37

talk shows, 103–105
Tamerius, K. L., 5, 89
targeted Member, 37
Theilmann, John, 27
Theriault, Sean, 136
Thomas, Sue, 5, 26, 28, 89

"token," 90, 121
trailblazers, 111
Tuesday Group, 135

Uhlaner, Carole, 102

Value Action Team, 135
Van Dyke, Vernon, 53
Vega, A., 51, 55
Voting Behavior, 44, 52, 55–56, 62, 64, 66–68, 106–107, 109, 129, 132, 134
Voting Rights Act, 28
vulnerability, 22, 49

Walker, Thomas G., 53–54
War on Terror, 106
Washington, D.C., 15–16
Watts, J.C., Jr., 101, 110, 116
Welch, Susan, 26–27, 51, 55
welfare debate, 58

whip team, 94–95, 97
widows, 30
Wilcox, Clyde, 26
Wilhite, Allen, 27
Wolfinger, Raymond E., 35
women's
    incorporation in the party organization, 80
    issues, 28, 55–56, 59, 75–76, 134
    participation in the party organization, 80
    status in the party organization, 80
Women's National Democratic Club, 11

Year of the Woman, The, 26, 30, 55
Yoder, Janice D., 90
Young, Bill, 7

Zipp, John F., 27, 127